After SANDY

ADVANCING
STRATEGIES
FOR
LONG-TERM
RESILIENCE
AND
ADAPTABILITY

About the Urban Land Institute

The Urban Land Institute is a nonprofit research and education organization whose mission is to provide leadership in the responsible use of land and in creating and sustaining thriving communities worldwide.

The Institute maintains a membership representing a broad spectrum of interests and sponsors a wide variety of educational programs and forums to encourage an open exchange of ideas and sharing of experience. ULI initiates research that anticipates emerging land use trends and issues, provides advisory services, and publishes a wide variety of materials to disseminate information on land use development.

Established in 1936, the Institute today has nearly 30,000 members and associates from some 92 countries, representing the entire spectrum of the land use and development disciplines. Professionals represented include developers, builders, property owners, investors, architects, public officials, planners, real estate brokers, appraisers, attorneys, engineers, financiers, academics, students, and librarians.

ULI relies heavily on the experience of its members. It is through member involvement and information resources that ULI has been able to set standards of excellence in development practice. The Institute is recognized internationally as one of America's most respected and widely quoted sources of objective information on urban planning, growth, and development.

COVER PHOTO: NASA

Recommended bibliographic listing:

Urban Land Institute. *After Sandy: Advancing Strategies for Long-Term Resilience and Adaptability*. Washington, DC: Urban Land Institute, 2013.

©2013 by the Urban Land Institute.

ISBN: 978-0-87420-292-2

About ULI
Advisory Services

The goal of ULI's Advisory Services program is to bring the finest expertise in the real estate field to bear on complex land use planning and development projects, programs, and policies. Since 1947, this program has assembled well over 600 ULI-member teams to help sponsors find creative, practical solutions for issues such as downtown redevelopment, land management strategies, evaluation of development potential, growth management, community revitalization, brownfields redevelopment, military base reuse, provision of low-cost and affordable housing, and asset management strategies, among other matters. A wide variety of public, private, and nonprofit organizations have contracted for ULI's advisory services.

Each panel team is composed of highly qualified professionals who volunteer their time to ULI. They are chosen for their knowledge of the panel topic and screened to ensure their objectivity. ULI's interdisciplinary panel teams provide a holistic look at development problems. A respected ULI member who has previous panel experience chairs each panel.

The agenda for a five-day panel assignment is intensive. It includes an in-depth briefing day composed of a tour of the site and meetings with sponsor representatives; a day of hour-long interviews of typically 50 to 75 key community representatives; and two days of formulating recommendations.

Long nights of discussion precede the panel's conclusions. On the final day on site, the panel typically makes an oral presentation of its findings and conclusions to the sponsor. A written report is prepared and published.

Because the sponsoring entities are responsible for significant preparation before the panel's visit, including sending extensive briefing materials to each member and arranging for the panel to meet with key local community members and stakeholders in the project under consideration, participants in ULI's five-day panel assignments are able to make accurate assessments of a sponsor's issues and to provide recommendations in a compressed amount of time.

A major strength of the program is ULI's unique ability to draw on the knowledge and expertise of its members, including land developers and owners, public officials, academics, representatives of financial institutions, and others. In fulfillment of the mission of the Urban Land Institute, the Advisory Services panel report is intended to provide objective advice that will promote the responsible use of land to enhance the environment.

Acknowledgments

The panel wishes to thank the many individuals who assisted with this process, especially James J. Florio, former New Jersey governor; Brian Fishman of Palantir Technologies; Cas Holloway, the New York City deputy mayor for operations; Joshua Murphy, from the Digital Coast Initiative of the National Oceanic and Atmospheric Administration; and Henk Ovink, senior adviser to Secretary of Housing and Urban Development Shaun Donovan in

his role as chair of the federal Hurricane Sandy Rebuilding Task Force. These five individuals briefed the panel and provided context and a clear sense of the challenges, and prepared it well for its work.

The panel also extends its gratitude to the more than 100 interviewees who contributed time and insights to this process. Thanks also go to the many individuals who served as tour guides for the panel, providing time and insight. Representing a diverse and informed public, these stakeholders, with their passion and understanding, provided valuable information and perspectives, greatly aiding the panel in its analysis.

PROJECT STAFF

Kathleen Carey
Executive Vice President and
    Chief Content Officer

Gayle Berens
Senior Vice President
Education and Advisory Group

Thomas Eitler
Vice President
Advisory Services Program

John K. McIlwain
Senior Resident Fellow/
    J. Ronald Terwilliger
    Chair for Housing

Annie Finkenbinder Best
Director
Advisory Services Program

Daniel Lobo
Manager, Awards
Education and Advisory Group

Katrina Flora
Intern

James Mulligan
Managing Editor

Joanne Platt
Publications Professionals LLC
Manuscript Editor

Betsy VanBuskirk
Creative Director

John Hall
John Hall Design Group
Book and Cover Designer

Craig Chapman
Senior Director
Publishing Operations

Kathryn Craig
Associate
Advisory Services Program

Contents

TOP: Hurricane Sandy damage north of Seaside Heights, New Jersey. **BOTTOM:** Sandy left the JetStar roller coaster in Seaside Heights in the Atlantic Ocean.

AFTER SANDY: ADVANCING STRATEGIES FOR LONG-TERM RESILIENCE AND ADAPTABILITY

Introduction

Hurricane Sandy was the worst natural disaster ever to hit the New York–New Jersey region. When it landed on October 29, 2012, the region was unprepared for its impact despite years of reports and warnings that an event like Sandy was a probability in the near future. Climate experts are now saying that although many aspects of Sandy were unique, the region will likely experience events of its magnitude with increasing frequency in the decades ahead.

Adding to the ferocity of the storms expected in the future is the seemingly inexorable rise in sea levels, a major challenge for coastal regions around the world. The most recent projections estimate that sea levels will rise in New York City in the range of 20 to 36 inches by 2100.[1] The National Oceanic and Atmospheric Administration's map of sea level rise shows clearly that many of the most vulnerable areas in New York and New Jersey were fortunate to have avoided the worst consequences of Sandy, while some seemingly safe areas were caught in Sandy's relatively unusual trajectory. This outcome points to the extraordinary unpredictability of major weather events and underscores the fact that long-term planning must be based on assessing the risk or potential for harm in the future, not on the degree of damage caused by past events.

In short, climate change is here to stay, though how severe it may become depends on our ability as humans to mitigate its causes and to create resilient communities that can absorb its impact and continue to thrive and grow. Most urban regions

THIS PAGE, FROM LEFT: ANTON OPARIN; JAYDENSONBX; ULI; NEW YORK AIR NATIONAL GUARD, TECH. SGT. JEREMY M. CALL. FACING PAGE, FROM TOP: GOVERNOR'S OFFICE/TIM LARSEN; ANTHONY QUINTANO

3

around the world are especially vulnerable to these changes. That vulnerability makes the need for evaluating and implementing longer-term strategies for resilience and preparedness in those regions critical today. This need is all the more true given their growing economic, social, and environmental value as the world becomes more urbanized.

BACKGROUND

The New York–New Jersey region has an unusually complex mix of land use patterns that must be taken into account when considering long-term resilience for the region. No one solution can possibly be appropriate for high-density land that is also very high in value (such as Lower Manhattan) and low-density areas with moderate land values (such as Long Beach or the smaller communities along the Staten Island and New Jersey shorelines). In between these extremes is a wide mix of more urban and less urban coastal communities.

Tying this region together is a complex system of infrastructure. Although the region's infrastructure is aging, it still makes up one of the most extensive, dense, and heavily invested systems in the United States. It is a critical component to the region's role as one of the most significant economic centers in

the nation. As an international center of finance and commerce, what happens in the greater New York–New Jersey region is key to the strategic economic advantage of the country.

Among the many challenges this situation presents is the need to prepare the region's complex physical, economic, and government systems for this new reality. To that end, the Urban Land Institute (ULI) planned and held a disaster assistance Advisory Services panel (see feature box) to consider how best to develop the long-term resilience and preparedness needed by the region if it is to continue to prosper in this new future successfully. Over its long history, ULI has convened many such panels, bringing a unique perspective to bear on what is needed to best plan for rebuilding after catastrophic events.

The New York–New Jersey region mobilized quickly, and within the year a host of plans has been developed to rebuild the region. Indeed, many plans existed before Hurricane Sandy that were intended to guide the region in preparing for events like Sandy, the second costliest hurricane in U.S. history. These reports, issued both before and after Sandy hit, make up a rich body of recommendations. Although many are quite consistent, some are in conflict, and there also appear to be some gaps in

SEA LEVEL RISE AND COASTAL FLOODING IMPACTS

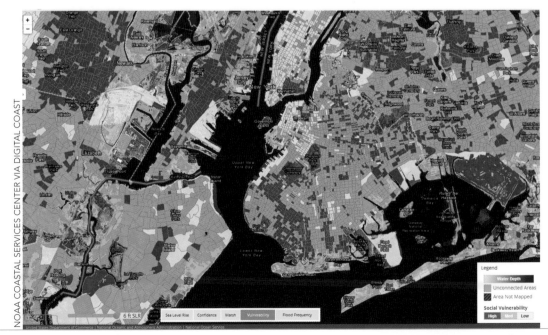

NOAA COASTAL SERVICES CENTER VIA DIGITAL COAST

some reports. All of these reports were reviewed by ULI and taken into account by the ULI Advisory Services panel in making its recommendations.

THE PANEL'S PROCESS

This post-Sandy panel was unique for ULI because it was convened without a specific sponsor. Instead, it was initiated by three ULI district councils—ULI New York, ULI Northern New Jersey, and ULI Philadelphia, with the support of the head office in Washington, D.C.—and paid for by the ULI Foundation.

The 25 members of the team were carefully chosen for their expertise and for their representation of various geographic areas. Thus, they represented a broad range of expertise in the infrastructure, design, real estate development, finance and investment, and public policy professions and included climate change and sustainability experts, from both local ULI New York and New Jersey membership as well as national and international leadership.

The panel began work on Sunday, July 14, with a briefing of the program, followed by a boat tour to view the Manhattan, Brooklyn, and Queens shorelines, as well as the Jersey City and Hoboken shores. That evening, the panelists heard remarks from former New Jersey governor James J. Florio, as well as the story of a dramatic innovation in technology to support recovery workers from Brian Fishman of Palantir Technologies.

On Monday, the panel heard from speakers: Cas Holloway, the New York City deputy mayor for operations who oversaw the development of Mayor Bloomberg's comprehensive report on rebuilding New York City post-Sandy; Joshua Murphy, from the Digital Coast Initiative of the National Oceanic and Atmospheric Administration (NOAA); and Henk Ovink, senior adviser to Secretary of Housing and Urban Development Shaun Donovan in his role as chair of the federal Hurricane Sandy Rebuilding Task Force.

The panel members then separated into teams to tour various areas of the region: Long Island and Queens (Breezy Point, the Rockaways, Long Beach, and Garden City); the eastern shores of Staten Island and New Jersey (including the northern New Jersey beaches down to Long Branch); and Lower Manhattan, Brooklyn, Hoboken, and Jersey City.

The following day, the panel conducted over 100 interviews with local residents, politicians, climate change experts, developers, designers, and so forth,

in three locations. The interviews are a critical part of the panel process because they provide a context and a range of viewpoints to help the panelists better understand the many reports and studies they reviewed in advance of the panel. The interviews

ULI ADVISORY SERVICES PANELS

ULI Advisory Services has a history of helping communities develop effective strategies to recover from floods, hurricanes, tornadoes, bridge collapses, and manmade disasters. Panels help communities address a wide range of immediate and long-term postdisaster questions and strategies. All ULI panel teams include professionals with diverse points of view—engineers, developers, planners, designers, investors, market analysts, and public officials—who volunteer their time and work together for six days to generate grounded, innovative solutions.

In 2009, for example, ULI was asked to go to Cedar Rapids, Iowa, to provide a focused, strategic look at a specific portion of the city—the area in and around the U.S. Cellular Center in downtown—and to offer strategies for redeveloping and revitalizing the

downtown core near the center after the flood.

ULI has held several panels along the Gulf Coast in response to Hurricanes Katrina and Ike, including in Galveston, Texas; Pascagoula, Mississippi; Bayou La Batre, Alabama; the Mississippi Gulf Coast; and most notably New Orleans. These communities faced (and are still grappling with) some of the same rebuilding issues that the New York–New Jersey region is coping with in the wake of Sandy. The extent of collaboration with local leaders and subsequent adoption of the panels' recommendations has varied. And in some cases, the recommendations have led to public controversy, often because of the pragmatic approach the panels take. The lessons learned from these past panels significantly helped shape the panelists' work through this panel and report.

ULI'S WORK IN COASTAL DEVELOPMENT ISSUES

ULI is not a newcomer to working on issues surrounding coastal disasters and resilience. In addition to having conducted numerous disaster assistance Advisory Services panels, in 2007 ULI published *Ten Principles for Coastal Development* in response to the 2004 and 2005 hurricane seasons that hammered Alabama, Florida, Louisiana, Mississippi, Texas, and other states. The 2005 hurricane season alone was ruinous, recording 2,280 deaths and damage totaling over $100 billion. The *Ten Principles* publication grew out of ULI's awareness that continued population growth, land development, and resort development were bringing more intense pressure to vulnerable areas, and that standard practices used to stabilize shorelines often disrupt the natural process-

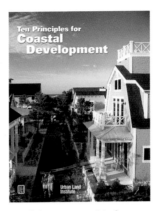

es of the coast and in fact exacerbate erosion as well as destroy natural habitats.

Although most of *Ten Principles for Coastal Development* focused on areas that are not especially densely populated, the principles are as true for the New York–New Jersey region as they are for lower-density regions:

1. Enhance value by protecting and conserving natural systems.

2. Identify natural hazards and reduce vulnerability.

3. Apply comprehensive assessments to the region and site.

4. Lower risk by exceeding standards for siting and construction.

5. Adopt successful practices from dynamic coastal conditions.

6. Use market-based incentives to encourage appropriate development.

7. Address social and economic equity concerns.

8. Balance the public's right of access and use with private property rights.

9. Protect fragile water resources on the coast.

10. Commit to stewardship that will sustain coastal areas.

In January 2013, as a precursor to the post-Sandy panel, ULI convened an interdisciplinary group of market stakeholders to explore the implications of new environmental risks in coastal regions on real estate practices and markets. That leadership dialogue amplified ULI's ongoing engagement in the issues of coastal planning, climate change, and postdisaster community rebuilding and gave shape to future research and programs across ULI's member networks. In addition to individuals representing the diversity of the real estate industry, forum participants included professionals from the insurance industry, government, and nonprofit organizations. The report of this convening, *Risk & Resilience in Coastal Regions*, summarizes the dialogue from the forum and identifies eight themes for future study. The report is intended to help frame a broader set of activities that will likely engage many coastal communities for some time.

also better connect them to what the individuals living in these areas actually faced after Sandy.

The group spent the next several days working on four broad sets of issues: (a) land use and development; (b) infrastructure, technology, and capacity; (c) finance, investment, and insurance; and (d) leadership and governance. This report represents the consensus of the panel about issues that should be considered in planning for the long-term resilience and preparedness of the New York–New Jersey region, and about ways to identify risks and develop strategies to prepare it for the future. The panel expects that much of what is contained in these recommendations will be of value to other regions around the country and abroad that are similarly challenged by climate change and rising sea levels.

Unlike many other ULI panels, this exercise did not focus on one specific site or project. By taking into account the extensive work already done or under way by local, state, and federal agencies, or other research and planning completed by nongovernmental organizations, the ULI panel chose to review several of the major plans and recommendations and to add whatever additional insights the panelists developed during a week of tours, interviews, conversations, and debates.

Key issues arose throughout the panel discussions that offered a broader approach to thinking about resiliency planning and how to address these issues within a community, city, or region. This report outlines an approach to assessing a region's preparedness and risk in the face of a disaster and offers tools that could be used to help prepare and strengthen a region. These recommendations are made to multiple audiences—state and city government, and the financial private sector—or in some cases, just one—the federal government. By developing this framework based on Hurricane Sandy as a case study, and targeting multiple audiences, this report is intended to address the New York–New Jersey region in the aftermath of Hurricane Sandy and also to be employed by other regions at risk. It can be used by communities to address issues specific to their region, as well as to help inform state and national policy setting. Ideally, this report and approach will help the conversation evolve and will be used to further refine the understanding of and techniques used in addressing resiliency in cities.

WHAT IS RESILIENCE?

BOUNCING BACK: "Resilience" has become a widely used term as people consider the needs of society to plan for the impact of the changing climate. Unfortunately, its meaning is often misunderstood because there are several types of resilience. A common concept of resilience comes from the way in which engineers use the term, which to them means the degree to which a structure can return to its original state after being stressed. Used in this way, it refers to the capacity of a community to recover after a disaster and to return to its state before the event. This concept is frequently referred to as the ability to "bounce back" and is often what community residents in hard-hit areas wish for most. In other words, a natural and common response to catastrophe is the desire to rebuild and restore what existed before the event. This desire often ignores the need and opportunity to rebuild in a way that reduces or eliminates the risk of the same damage recurring during another weather event.

BOUNCING FORWARD: Another way of looking at resilience is the ability not only to bounce back but also to "bounce forward"—to recover and at the same time to enhance the capacities of the community or organization to better withstand future stresses.

"In this way of thinking, then, resilient communities, people, and systems have the ability to thrive, improve, or reorganize themselves in a healthy way in response to stress; that is, they are less vulnerable to breakdown in the face of shocks and stress. . . . [R]esilient systems, communities, or people recover their normal states more quickly after stress and are capable of enduring greater stress. They demonstrate greater adaptive capacity and can maintain 'system functions' in the event of disturbances. This capacity applies to the ability to withstand acute, immediate, and sudden stresses as well as long-term chronic challenges.

Most discussions of resilience agree that it is a multifaceted concept and should be understood and measured across multiple social dimensions, including physical, social, economic, institutional, and ecological fronts."[a]

There are certain qualities that most experts in the field consider essential for the development of resilience in urban regions. Any urban region is a system made up of many parts, many of which themselves are systems. Given the human capacity to change and adapt in the face of challenges and changing circumstances, these regions can be considered to be what is known in systems theory as complex adaptive systems.

"In Complex Adaptive Systems, three key properties contribute to resilience:

"Diversity and Redundancy. The functioning and adaptive capacity of the system does not depend on any single component, community, or individual, and multiple parts of the system can substitute if one component fails.

"Modular Networks. The system comprises multiple smaller systems that are relatively independent of each other, complement each other, to a certain degree replicate each other, and are buffered from each other to minimize the transmission of shocks. Connections between subunits are necessary to enable the system to function as a whole, but structures exist to prevent the propagation of failures.

"Responsive, Regulatory Feedbacks. Structures or processes exist to transmit learning throughout the system. These feedback loops must be horizontal and vertical to maximize adaptability. Feedback loops must be understood as broadly as possible; for example, to include social-ecological feedback loops as well as feedback loops within traditional social or governance systems."[b]

a. Judith Rodin and Robert Garris, "Reconsidering Resilience for the 21st Century." In *USAID Frontiers in Development*, edited by Rajiv Shah and Steven Radelet (Washington, DC: U.S. Agency for International Development, 2012), PDF e-book, pp. 110–11.

b. Ibid., pp. 114–15.

TOP: HafenCity in Hamburg, Germany, the largest inner-city development in Europe, is near large expanses of water. Rather than being surrounded by dikes, all new buildings in HafenCity have been elevated on plinths made of mounds of compacted fill (*Warften* in German) designed to withstand the most extreme flooding.
BOTTOM: A Sandy panel member reviews briefing materials.

AFTER SANDY: ADVANCING STRATEGIES FOR LONG-TERM RESILIENCE AND ADAPTABILITY

Summary of Recommendations

The 25-person ULI panel made 23 specific recommendations, which are summarized below and explained in more detail in the sections following. The recommendations presented by the panel were derived from a multidisciplinary perspective. As multidisciplinary as the backgrounds of the panelists, these recommendations and their interdependent roles among four themes (land use and development; infrastructure, technology, and capacity; finance, investment, and insurance; and leadership and governance) also rely heavily on collaboration between disciplines and stakeholders. Though not exhaustive, these recommendations hit on major challenges facing regions and some innovative methods for addressing them. There is no unilateral, standard approach to this topic; these tools and policy changes are steps that must often be taken in conjunction with one another and will constantly evolve with new information. The nature of this Advisory Services panel process dictates that the recommendations tend to be more strategic in nature and less precise and detailed than some communities may expect, but this approach also allows flexibility in adapting the recommendations to the local situation. That assumption is reflected in the recommendations below.

Land Use and Development

RECOMMENDATION 1

RECONSTITUTE THE HURRICANE SANDY REBUILDING TASK FORCE AS AN ONGOING RESILIENCE TASK FORCE AND USE IT AS A MODEL FOR OTHER REGIONS.

The main objective of the Hurricane Sandy Rebuilding Task Force is to drive and ensure "cabinet-level, government-wide, and region-wide coordination to help communities as they are making decisions about long-term rebuilding."[2] The task force should be reconstituted as a continuing resilience task force composed of federal representatives and representatives from New York state and New Jersey. The federal representatives would have the authority and mandate to identify, prioritize, and allocate funds for major infrastructure in the region in consultation with the state and city representatives. The panel believes that there is a need for high-level coordinated leadership for project prioritization and resource allocation.

RECOMMENDATION 2

PROMOTE REGIONAL COORDINATION.

Interconnected infrastructure networks are regional in scope, but they also have neighborhood-by-neighborhood impacts. A change in the way local governments organize themselves is needed to build an infrastructure framework that is flexible, that is sensitive to community context, and that supports the development of capacity for local disaster planning and response decision making. Coastal protection demands cooperation among people and governments that share geomorphology. Without well-informed collective decision making about priorities and methods, major new coastal works will be realized slowly if at all, and their effectiveness will be reduced.

RECOMMENDATION 3

IDENTIFY THOSE PARTS OF THE REGION TO PROTECT AND INVEST IN THAT ARE CRITICAL TO THE REGIONAL ECONOMY, CULTURE, AND HEALTH, SAFETY, AND WELFARE.

Every region has areas that are of special importance to its economic vitality and well-being. In addition, there are areas that are essential to its health and welfare, and to its unique cultural and historic heritage. An essential task of regional coordination is to identify these priority areas for protection and investment long term, given that resources are finite and all desirable projects cannot be undertaken.

RECOMMENDATION 4

IDENTIFY LOCAL LAND USE TYPOLOGIES IN ORDER TO ASSESS THE BUILT ENVIRONMENT FOR RESILIENCY.

The first step in determining a region's capacity for resiliency and in developing and implementing the right tools to improve that capacity is to conduct an assessment of existing land use typologies and local resources to determine the unique vulnerability of each. Identifying typologies requires taking into account many factors, including environmental, political, cultural, and economic conditions, as well as the locality's density, transit access, scale, and so forth. The ability of the region to prepare and respond to future events is really the sum of the abilities of each of its localities.

RECOMMENDATION 5

USE DEFINED LAND TYPOLOGIES IN A COST/BENEFIT ANALYSIS TO IDENTIFY LESS VULNERABLE "VALUE ZONES" FOR LONG-TERM PLANNING AND PUBLIC SPENDING.

Climate change's impacts have forced many communities to rethink the ways in which their land is used. Many are facing the politically challenging task of balancing the desire to continue existing land uses for homes and businesses with often dramatic increases in the costs of protecting and rebuilding those structures determined to be at risk. In responding to the costs of preserving and protecting certain high-risk locations, communities will need to develop new land use overlay zones that balance the value of

continuing their current use with the cost of doing so. As jurisdictions in coastal regions face this reality, over time it will lead to new policies, investment strategies, and outcomes that will shift investment from high-risk areas to those less vulnerable.

Infrastructure, Technology, and Capacity

RECOMMENDATION 6

DEVELOP A REGIONAL INFRASTRUCTURE VISION, REVIEW IT REGULARLY, AND SET PRIORITIES.

It is essential that a vision of a comprehensive infrastructure framework be created that relates to the growing demand and unique physical characteristics of the region as a coherent whole, not as a series of independent parts. Because funding will never be sufficient for designing and rebuilding all elements of the region's comprehensive infrastructure system at once, priorities need to be set regionally for which systems need upgrading for resilience first.

RECOMMENDATION 7

CONSIDER LONG-TERM RESILIENCY WHEN EVALUATING REBUILDING STRATEGIES.

The available financial resources for capital investments fall short of what is needed for the proposed resiliency and protection projects. Cost/benefit analysis of infrastructure investments is an excellent tool for regional decision makers to use in order to comprehensively evaluate the implementation strategies of long-term resiliency. To select a rational sequence and strategy for implementing resiliency measures, criteria for prioritization need to be established that include a cost/benefit assessment of criticality of need, protection of market value, and potential market value to be created, among other factors.

The firm dlandstudio partnered with ARO to create "A New Urban Ground" for the Museum of Modern Art's 2010 "Rising Currents" exhibition, calling attention to Manhattan's vulnerability to climate change impacts. A combination of strategies, including perimeter wetlands, a raised edge, and sponge slips paired with new upland street infrastructure systems, protect the island from flooding in the event of a large storm. The proposed porous streets and a graduated edge form an interconnected system.

RECOMMENDATION 8

DESIGN PROTECTIVE INFRASTRUCTURE TO DO MORE THAN PROTECT.

A significant allocation of public resources has been made to infrastructure that is created both to improve resiliency and to increase the competitiveness of the region. Since protective infrastructure can serve multiple functions, it can be of great economic and ecological value if it is designed in a way that contributes to the creation of new development opportunities, doubles up to accommodate other infrastructure uses, improves the quality of the public realm and waterfront experience, and enhances natural systems.

RECOMMENDATION 9

EXPLORE THE POTENTIAL OF SOFT SYSTEMS.

A multifunctional approach to infrastructure can occur through soft (use of natural and landscape systems) and hard infrastructure design. As the re-gion begins to carefully consider its infrastructure network as a tool for resiliency and recovery, it is well positioned to be on the forefront of integrating more soft infrastructure into the overall system. Incorporating soft infrastructure can be a cost-effective way to build systems that protect the region's 520 miles of coastline.

RECOMMENDATION 10

ALLOW FOR SAFE FAILURE OF SOME NONCRITICAL INFRASTRUCTURE SYSTEMS.

Certain elements of the region's infrastructure, although important, can be allowed to fail. Short-term interruptions of these systems can be permitted and planned for to allow more investment and support for life and safety critical systems.

RECOMMENDATION 11

CREATE INFRASTRUCTURE RECOVERY PLANS FOR QUICK PARTIAL SERVICE RESTORATION.

Priorities for restoration should be set by stakeholders, and the infrastructure system should be, to the extent possible, designed to accommodate those priorities quickly in the wake of a disaster. This objective could be approached through stages of restoration that focus on bringing power back to high-priority infrastructure first.

RECOMMENDATION 12

ENCOURAGE INDIVIDUAL PREPAREDNESS DURING SHORT-TERM INFRASTRUCTURE OUTAGES.

Those in areas at risk for power outage, transportation limitation, or property damage should be ready for a wide range of system disruptions in the case of a disaster. The public should not presume that infrastructure systems will operate perfectly post-disaster. To prepare, citizens will require reliable, frequent, and timely distribution of information from the public sector. Historically, social networks and community-based organizations (CBOs) have been the most successful providers of immediate relief after a disaster and are often a secondary source of ongoing relief. For relief to be possible, these organizations need to be prepared with goods to support the needs during power outages and other interruptions.

Finance, Investment, and Insurance

RECOMMENDATION 13

IMPLEMENT CREATIVE EXTRAMUNICIPAL FINANCING MECHANISMS.

Because of the magnitude of capital requirements and the frequently multijurisdictional scope of many infrastructure improvements, these projects can only be undertaken by federal or state agencies in cooperation with local municipalities or through a regional authority empowered to raise capital. At the present time, there is a gap in funding sources for resiliency infrastructure projects. Thus, it is incumbent upon states to coordinate and create their own resiliency funding authorities.

RECOMMENDATION 14

REVISE FEDERAL FUNDING ASSISTANCE TO ALLOW LOCAL DISCRETION AND DIRECT FUNDING FLOWS TO COMMUNITIES WHEN POSSIBLE.

Storm recovery money from the federal government comes with designated specific uses that limit the flexibility of towns and cities in spending to improve multiple infrastructures simultaneously. Frequently, federal assistance funds singular, single-use projects. There are too many nondiscretionary resources and too few human resources to integrate them effectively in this manner. If federal assistance were more flexible, infrastructure investments would be more powerful and would more effectively serve the communities in which they are made.

RECOMMENDATION 15

PROVIDE SMALL COMMUNITIES WITH FINANCIAL SUPPORT TO REPLACE LOST LOCAL TAX DOLLARS.

Consideration should be given to a state disaster and financing mechanism to offset the loss of property taxes in communities that restrict redevelopment of sites where properties have been destroyed and instead to allow communities to dedicate the land to public purposes, such as natural infrastructure. As part of this proposed program, any turnover of land whose cost is offset in this way should be deeded for public use in perpetuity.

RECOMMENDATION 16

ACCURATELY PRICE CLIMATE RISK INTO PROPERTY VALUE AND INSURANCE.

Risk must be priced accurately. That said, much more study and information are required, especially with respect to flood insurance, as scientific and engineering understanding of flood risk is rapidly evolving. Insurance pricing should be examined to determine whether market distortions are occurring because of misunderstanding of climate events; there are certain areas outside the region where insurance premiums have increased in response to climate events for types of insurance coverage that are not directly affected by such events. Furthermore, certain insurance markets still require federal backstops, both for catastrophic risk and to support a graduated transition for lower-income communities to full risk pricing.

RECOMMENDATION 17

ALLOW PARTIAL COMPLIANCE AND MITIGATION MEASURES IN ORDER TO CREATE FLEXIBILITY IN INSURANCE PREMIUMS.

Appropriate reductions in premiums should be considered in flood mitigation programs even if properties fail to fully meet local, Federal Emergency Management Agency (FEMA), or flood insurance requirements. These measures may be appropriate in circumstances in which it is impossible or prohibitively expensive to raise the elevation of the building or to implement other zoning requirements. Integrating careful assessment of the value of flood mitigation efforts should also encourage investment in retrofits, which can reduce the impact (cost, duration, displacement) of future extreme climate events and thereby protect major private market investments.

RECOMMENDATION 18

DESIGN FINANCING TO HELP RELIEVE THE RECOVERY BURDEN FOR LOW-INCOME HOUSEHOLDS AND SMALL BUSINESSES.

Lower-income households—both homeowners and renters—and small businesses without substantial savings are disadvantaged in financing their recovery. There are a number of possible financing mechanisms that federal, state, and local authorities might consider to finance or relieve some of this burden. It is vital, however, that subsidies and tax abatements do not distort individuals' or businesses' decision-making process on whether or how to rebuild in certain areas. Individuals and communities need to rebuild, but that does not mean that all rebuilding should necessarily be subsidized. Any

subsidies or tax abatements provided by the government should be strategically targeted to designated value zones or other circumstances where rebuilding is a priority.

Leadership and Governance

RECOMMENDATION 19

DEVOLVE FUNDING TO THE LOWEST EFFECTIVE LEVEL WHERE APPROPRIATE.

Resources should be devolved to the lowest level of government—such as village, township, or city—that can demonstrate capacity to both manage and implement these funds and coordinate decision making within the region.

RECOMMENDATION 20

ENHANCE THE CAPACITY FOR COORDINATION AND COLLABORATION AMONG DIFFERENT LEVELS OF GOVERNMENT—FROM LOCAL TO FEDERAL.

To promote regional cooperation among diverse localities while preserving the autonomy and character of the latter, the panel recommends that the federal and state governments provide clear incentives to encourage regional cooperation. The lowest level of government—such as village, township, or city—should both manage and implement these funds and coordinate decision making with the regional entity, if it can demonstrate capacity to do so. The panel recommends that the federal and state governments provide clear incentives to encourage cooperation among neighboring localities to create local planning clusters.

RECOMMENDATION 21

BUILD CAPACITY FOR DECISION MAKING AT THE LOCAL LEVEL.

Many localities lack capacity and need greater access to information and resources, as well as the support of coordinating entities at higher levels of government. Resources and expertise from other levels of government must have greater duration and continuity than they do currently. Information systems and sharing agreements among coastal communities are needed, and they can be facilitated by or encouraged by a federal or regional coordinating body. The federal government needs to institute, and make permanent, a series of training sessions for local governments to teach them how to prepare for and respond to disasters. These sessions should include both elected officials and key staff.

RECOMMENDATION 22

CREATE PROGRAMS TO PROVIDE KNOWLEDGE SHARING AND PROFESSIONAL TRAINING.

As communities start to rebuild and plan for a resilient future, climate change is a factor that must be incorporated into education, training, and professional practices. The entire professional spectrum of advisers, whom communities and individuals rely on for professional services—including architects, engineers, planners, design professionals, surveyors, and appraisers, as well as investment professionals who contribute to the underlying analysis of investment decisions—must be technically expert in areas that will be integral to decision making and implementation of both mitigation and resilient strategies and practices.

RECOMMENDATION 23

MAKE CRITICAL INFORMATION EASILY UNDERSTANDABLE AND READILY ACCESSIBLE BOTH DURING AND AFTER A DISASTER.

The politics of difficult decisions can paralyze a community, or it can create the collective will to change. The ability to provide a series of grounded facts and to create an environment in which discussion of these facts and their consequences can take place enhances the probability of change. The long-term resiliency of the coast depends on hundreds of thousands of individual decisions by property owners—some in beach communities and some in urban neighborhoods. The quality of those decisions will depend in large part on good information. The critical information that people need to make informed decisions—such as base flood elevations, availability of funding, the cost of insurance, the availability of buyouts, building codes that will be required in flood areas, and the NOAA maps of projected sea level rise—is often not easily understood or attainable by individuals but is essential to sound decision making.

The Battery Park underpass was filled with more than 12 feet of water during Hurricane Sandy.

AFTER SANDY: ADVANCING STRATEGIES FOR LONG-TERM RESILIENCE AND ADAPTABILITY

Land Use and Development

Zoning codes, market trends, policy, and above all market value drive land use. Often dictated by the environmental condition and policy constraints, land is developed—and used—to maximize its market and social value. However, the long-term market value of a development is difficult to assess accurately, especially given the uncertain effects of the changing climate and the rising costs of long-term public subsidy of a particular land use in high-risk areas. The ability of planners, investors, lenders, and government leaders to make wise

long-term land use decisions is constrained by historic precedent, existing investment, and unsustainable market trends. Land use and development decision makers, whether at the individual, city, regional, state, or federal scale, need to be fully informed about the risk posed by the likely increase in natural disasters. Only in this way can they create effective long-term approaches to curbing current, detrimental land use trends and gradually adapt land use patterns in accordance with environmental shifts.

The first step in determining a region's capacity for resiliency, and in developing and implementing the right tools to improve that capacity, is to conduct an assessment of existing conditions and resources to determine the region's vulnerability. Throughout the panel process, the panelists routinely circled back to the large variety of land uses in the New York–New Jersey region. They noted how many unique land types were present, distinguished from one another by environmental, political,

THIS PAGE, FROM LEFT: JAYLAZARIN; ULI; CATHERINE LANE; KEVIN DOWNS. FACING PAGE, FROM TOP: MIKE STOBE/GETTY IMAGES; ANDREYGATASH

17

cultural, and financial issues. The ability of the region as a whole to cope with the effects of Sandy is the sum of the ability of each of these varying land uses. There needs to be a region-wide alignment of priority projects with measurable long-term public benefits to be weighed against current and future costs. Although billions of dollars have been allocated to the New York–New Jersey region post-Sandy, even that level of funding is still insufficient to build all the infrastructure necessary or desired for long-term resilience, especially if current land use patterns continue. Proper allocation of financial resources is vital to the recovery of the region, but it must also be prioritized and managed through a long-term, regional, comprehensive, and thorough approach.

RECOMMENDATION 1

RECONSTITUTE THE HURRICANE SANDY REBUILDING TASK FORCE AS AN ONGOING RESILIENCE TASK FORCE AND USE IT AS A MODEL FOR OTHER REGIONS.

When President Obama established the Hurricane Sandy Rebuilding Task Force in December 2012, he made a strong statement about what is needed to support effective rebuilding objectives based on the makeup of the task force. He included representatives from the Departments of the Treasury, the Interior, Agriculture, Commerce, Labor, Health and Human Services, Transportation, Energy, Education, Veterans Affairs, and Homeland Security, as well as the Environmental Protection Agency, the Small Business Administration, the Army Corps of Engineers, and eight other agencies. By so doing, the administration understood the need for taking a comprehensive look at vulnerabilities and risks and what is needed to strengthen resiliency in the broadest sense. The main objective of the task force was to drive and ensure "cabinet-level, government-wide, and region-wide coordination to help communities as they are making decisions about long-term rebuilding."[3] The task force also recently launched Rebuild by Design, a competition intended to generate innovative ideas and strategies from the private, nonprofit, and other sectors.

The panel recommends that lessons be taken from the Hurricane Sandy Rebuilding Task Force and that it be reconstituted as an ongoing resil-

ience task force. It should be composed of federal representatives and representatives from New York state and New Jersey. The federal representatives would have the authority and mandate to identify, prioritize, and allocate funds for major infrastructure in the region in consultation with the state and city representatives. Similar task forces should be set up in other vulnerable regions so that this structure is in place, dormant but ready to act, before an immediate need presents itself.

The panel believes that there is a need for high-level coordinated leadership for big decisions.

RECOMMENDATION 2

PROMOTE REGIONAL COORDINATION.

Interconnected infrastructure networks are regional in scope, but they also have neighborhood-by-neighborhood impacts. Infrastructure systems rarely share boundaries with political jurisdictions—water pipes do not stop at municipal borders—and thus a community cannot be resilient if its neighboring community is not. "Beyond-the-boundaries" planning and action are required for a robust system. Capital improvement plans vary between dense urban areas with existing capacity for planning and implementation, whereas smaller coastal communities may lack those resources. This disparity could create a weak link in the system because smaller communities might not realize how important their role is in implementing a broader plan that supports the goal of systemic infrastructure. A change in the way governments organize themselves is needed to build an infrastructure framework that is flexible, that is sensitive to community context, and that supports communities that need it in building capacity for decision making.

Coastal protection demands cooperation among people and governments that share geomorphology. Without collective decision making about priorities and methods, major new coastal waterworks will be realized slowly if at all, and their effectiveness will be reduced. Incremental investments can have unintended consequences. For example, breakwaters and reefs that cause storm surge waves to break offshore before they reach land, dunes that absorb wave energy, and seawalls and levees that seal out water are vastly more effective when they

Yellow cabs in a parking lot in Hoboken, New Jersey, were among an estimated 210,000 vehicles damaged in the New York–New Jersey region by the hurricane.

are long and unbroken. Breaks in continuity concentrate wave energy and water mass on the people who live in the breach. There are huge equity implications of communities engaging in these types of investments and shunting water to their disorganized or underfunded neighbors.

These are just two examples that make the case for the need for coordination to identify potential alliances, broker transfers of money for regional or local collaborations, and more effectively bring government and the private sector together to improve data organization and efficiently build high-quality infrastructure. Integrated infrastructure design depends on a less balkanized approach to design and implementation of major projects. In practice, design and delivery of infrastructure are often mired in overly participatory projects that require multiple layers of bureaucratic approvals. Or at the other extreme, sometimes the delivery of critical coastal projects is in the hands of a single, overstretched behemoth government entity. The coordinating entity should be charged with guiding the way money is

invested in infrastructure at federal, state, and local levels in ways that support the systemic vision.

RECOMMENDATION 3

IDENTIFY THOSE PARTS OF THE REGION TO PROTECT AND INVEST IN THAT ARE CRITICAL TO THE REGIONAL ECONOMY, CULTURE, AND HEALTH, SAFETY, AND WELFARE.

Every region has areas that are of special importance to its economic vitality and well-being. It also has areas that are essential to its health and welfare, and to its unique cultural and historic heritage. An essential task of regional coordination is to identify these priority areas for protection and investment long term. Often, views differ on which areas may be the most significant, but the leadership of the region needs to address this important priority setting through an open and public process.

The panel did not make specific recommendations regarding which areas of the New York–New Jersey region were the most valuable from this perspective. That said, the consensus was that areas like Lower Manhattan and Jersey City, vulnerable as they are to the rise in sea levels and to future storms, are central to the economy of the region and to the United States as a whole. An area like the Hunts Point food market (see feature box) is of particular value to the health and well-being of the region because more than 60 percent of all of the region's food passes through it. The other vulnerable but particularly high-value areas in a region would be determined by a regional, coordinated assessment.

RECOMMENDATION 4

IDENTIFY LOCAL LAND USE TYPOLOGIES IN ORDER TO ASSESS THE BUILT ENVIRONMENT FOR RESILIENCY.

To begin assessing the existing built environment for resiliency, it is important to recognize and identify the wide variation in the types of communities that could be affected by weather events. By recognizing typologies and their varying scales, characters, and economic and natural resources, a framework can be developed for evaluating investment and resource priorities, as well as recommending required policy changes. Whether strengthening growth management policies in order to condense urban areas, to conserve critical environmental resources, and to compact necessary infrastructure (and protection) investments, or improving stormwater management on all new developments to reduce overall runoff and lessen the impacts of major storms, land use and development decisions are based on the identified local typology and constraints.

The panel began by identifying land use typologies for the New York–New Jersey region. Both these typologies and their definitions will differ in other regions because each has its own unique characteristics. Determining the region's various land use typologies is essential, however, because a comprehensive cost/benefit analysis of investments for long-term preparedness and resilience can only be based on

Marines from the Eighth Engineer Support Battalion, Second Marine Logistics Group, aided the National Guard and FEMA in humanitarian operations in Breezy Point, New York.

AFTER SANDY: ADVANCING STRATEGIES FOR LONG-TERM RESILIENCE AND ADAPTABILITY

each land typology and land use value. This method is ultimately the best way to determine "value zones"—those areas in a region that warrant continued public reinvestment and future development.

Identifying typologies involves a conglomeration of characteristics, such as density, transit access, scale, and so forth. Determining a typology is not a simple one-size-fits-all exercise. Oftentimes, for example, high-density areas are distinguished by an intense mix of uses, transit accessibility, and a dominance of multifamily housing. With some exceptions, the water's edge in these locations is reserved for industrial or urban public recreation uses, such as parks, roads, and trails. Many of the very high density areas have significant resources and political capital, strong private market demand, and the high potential for continuing private investment. They are often communities with strong institutions: governments capable of managing complex administrative processes and strong and organized civic and business leadership. However, parts of these areas frequently have very limited resources and political capital and are in great need of public support.

In the New York–New Jersey region, many communities are highly urbanized. And although it is important to recognize that they are subject to the same impacts of sea level rise and climate change as more rural coastal communities, they frequently have more private resources and political capital to draw from to rebuild after events than less developed localities. The areas around Manhattan, for instance, including Jersey City, Brooklyn, and Queens, have been major national economic centers for centuries, and changing their land use today seems neither possible nor financially sound. As a result, both public and private investment should go into preparing and preserving Manhattan and its immediate environs for full productivity.

Many of the communities in the region, however, are primarily low- to medium-density residential, with commercial areas that range from tourist-serving hubs to main streets and suburban-style strip centers. The built environment and lifestyle in these communities are centered on the beach and other types of recreational water access. Single-family homes are typically on small lots and command much of the waterfront. These areas typically include a combination of low-lying environmentally sensitive areas, low-lying developed areas, and

The top of a lighthouse on Coney Island. The beloved amusement park suffered significant damage.

upland areas. Because of their low elevations, they are often plagued by a high groundwater table and poor drainage and are often susceptible to frequent flooding. They are among the most vulnerable areas in the region.

Social and economic forces also stress these most vulnerable areas. Because of their natural beauty and adjacency to the ocean, barrier islands are a popular destination for vacations and second homes. Local governance on the barrier islands is often part-time when a municipality is located entirely on the island, or full-time in cases where the barrier island is part of the municipality of the mainland. The limited space and lack of public services on these barrier islands often dictate the development intensity on the islands.

RECOMMENDATION 5

USE DEFINED LAND TYPOLOGIES IN A COST/BENEFIT ANALYSIS TO IDENTIFY LESS VULNERABLE "VALUE ZONES" FOR LONG-TERM PLANNING AND PUBLIC SPENDING.

Coastal communities across the region are being forced to rethink the ways in which their land is used. Many are facing the politically challenging task of balancing the desire to continue existing

Employees from the Metropolitan Transportation Authority worked to restore the South Ferry subway station after it was flooded by seawater during the hurricane.

land uses for homes and businesses with often dramatic increases in the costs of protecting and rebuilding those structures determined to be at risk. As communities respond to new land use constraints associated with location-based risk profiles, new land use overlay zones will emerge that take into account the fiscal balancing act of weighing the value proposition of delivering public benefits with the cost of those obligations. This is a new calculus that many jurisdictions in coastal regions will have to explore and that over time will lead to new policy and investment strategies and outcomes.

Already, existing land use zoning is being "overlaid" by new policy initiatives at the federal level. The goal of making the National Flood Insurance Program (NFIP) more actuarially sound motivated Congress to pass the Biggert-Waters Flood Insurance Reform Act in 2012 for a five-year term. The legislation requires an end to subsidies in the program that benefit certain properties, which are "pre-FIRM" (Flood Insurance Rate Map) and are typically paying artificially low rates that do not reflect actual flood risk. These properties include, among others, the following:

» Any residential property that is not the primary residence of an individual;

» Any severe repetitive-loss property;

» Any property that has incurred flood-related damages that cumulatively exceed the fair market value of the property;

» Any business property; and

» Any property that after the date of the bill has incurred substantial damage or has experienced "substantial improvement exceeding 30 percent of the fair market value of the property."[4]

FEMA categorizes about 75,000 coastal properties as having subsidized NFIP coverage in the coastal New Jersey and Long Island region, one of the highest concentrations of subsidized flood-insured properties in the country.[5]

FEMA administers the NFIP and is currently remapping special coastal hazard areas, including the following zones:

» VE—high-velocity impact areas directly at the shoreline;

» Coastal AE—areas outside of ocean surges, but within the limit of coastal wave action;

» AE—additional upland areas affected; and

» X—low-risk areas deemed not to be affected.

In addition, counties and some cities have instituted hurricane evacuation zones with a numerical nomenclature (1, 2, 3, 4, 5, 6) as in New York City and an alphabetical nomenclature (A, B, C, D, E) in counties that generally correlate to the categorization of hurricane strength by NOAA. Together, the update to the NFIP and the introduction of hurricane evacuation zones are introducing new decision criteria into land use planning frameworks. It is worth noting that these initiatives, at the federal and local jurisdictional level, do not factor in long-term sea-level-rise projections, which suggests that over time the decision criteria associated with place-based risk profiles will become more constrained than even the current revisions indicate.

The ULI panel discussed broader and longer-term land use scenarios that local jurisdictions might contemplate as they plan their long-term response to the changing climate and sea levels. These scenarios included the creation of possible new categories of coastal land use and infrastructure zones that would create new frameworks for public and private investment decisions (value zones). Among these categories might be the following:

» **Coastal Transition Zones**—areas where public subsidies and investments would be reduced or even halted and where public buyout funds would be created to allow private landowners

the opportunity to sell property to the public at a fair value. In these areas, the increased risk (and probability) of inclement events, which would also affect insurance rates, could cause the market value of these homes to significantly drop and could trap many residents in a financially unsustainable situation, when public subsidies and investments are reduced (or halted).

» **Coastal Impact Zones**—areas where public investment in infrastructure would be structured to explicitly allow for public standards of health, safety, and welfare to "fail" during times of storm or flood impact. The cost/benefit ratio in these areas does not promote rebuilding or additional investment, so that these areas would be evacuated, safely, but would not receive additional public support or funding. By providing a cushion, these areas function as "crumple zones" during high-impact events, and the loss of infrastructure would be specifically designed so it would not lead to other cascading impacts across metropolitan infrastructure systems.

» **Coastal Transformation Zones**—areas where public subsidies and investments would be targeted to transform an existing high-risk area of the built environment into a new urban design paradigm that included highly resilient measures, such as new hard and soft flood barriers and seawalls.

» **Smart Growth Receiving Zones**—areas in low-risk upland areas, which could be proactively dedicated as preferred areas of urban development and which facilitated the investment necessary to relocate populations and businesses in a manner that allowed for social continuity over time with low levels of market disruption.

TOP: Boardwalks along the shores of Long Island and New Jersey—including this one in Long Beach, New York—were shredded by Hurricane Sandy. **BOTTOM:** As of April 2013, the U.S. Army Corps of Engineers had handled nearly 1 million cubic yards of debris.

AFTER SANDY: ADVANCING STRATEGIES FOR LONG-TERM RESILIENCE AND ADAPTABILITY

Infrastructure, Technology, and Capacity

Infrastructure delivers the goods and services that ensure that communities are livable and continue to generate economic value, and so it is fundamental to increasing a community's ability to endure disruptions. Investment in infrastructure is also essential to preserving and encouraging the region's growth and the nation's competitiveness in the global economy. Because they constitute economic powerhouses, what happens in New York and New Jersey is critical to the strategic economic advantage of the country.

Thus, investing in infrastructure not only serves to protect the lives, health, and well-being of those living in the region, but it will also make the region more competitive for scarce public resources and more attractive for private investment. Infrastructure investment also has the inherent capacity to guide the location, quality, and accessibility of the region's growth and to guide its evolution to a greater resilience, increased vitality, and higher quality of life.

Despite concerns over aging infrastructure, the New York–New Jersey metropolitan area contains some of the most extensive, dense, and heavily invested-in infrastructure systems in the United States. Unfortunately, despite the need to repair that which was damaged and to plan for rebuilding in a more resilient fashion, the region's infrastructure (as well as that of most regions in the United States) already has a significant deficit in funding and needs substantial upgrading unconnected with

THIS PAGE, FROM LEFT: NYC DEPARTMENT OF TRANSPORTATION. GOVERNOR'S OFFICE/TIM LARSEN; NEIL R; ULI. **FACING PAGE, FROM TOP:** DAN DECHIARO; JAYDENSONBX

Located in the South Bronx, Hunts Point hosts one of the largest food distribution facilities in the world. Often referred to as "the food peninsula," this troubled neighborhood plays an essential role in the regional food supply. As the Sandy storm surge highlighted, careful attention must be paid to its operations during an emergency, and resources must be provided to guarantee efficient and sustained delivery of resources.

Located in a neighborhood of 45,000 people, Hunts Point food distribution facilities include the Produce and Meat Distribution Center, covering an area of 329 acres; the New York City Terminal Market, carrying fresh fruit and vegetables from 49 states and 55 foreign countries, with 475,000 square feet of warehouse space; the Hunts Point Cooperative Market, spreading over 38 acres; and the Fulton Fish Market

with 450,000 square feet. In aggregate, over 800 industrial businesses, employing over 25,000 workers, are located on the peninsula.

These markets are not public agencies; they are instead 42 businesses and tenants on land owned and managed by the New York City Economic Development Corporation (NYCEDC). Direct support from any level of government is mixed. A lot of attention has been paid to planning for disasters, but the ability of the markets to continue to fully operate long term during and after disasters is still problematic.

During the storm, distribution and energy supply issues emerged that threatened to endanger the ability of the markets to operate. For example, during Sandy's surge, the city-owned cofferdam on the Bronx River, which protects the riverside of the Hunts Point Terminal Produce Market (HPTPM), was close to flood-

During the storm, vast stocks of food were threatened by distribution and energy supply issues.

ADAM KUBAN

ing, which could have severely compromised operations at the HPTPM at the least. Although the HPTPM implemented measures to guarantee fuel supplies and to reinforce the security perimeter, it fortunately only lost power temporarily. A longer power outage would have compromised operations substantially.

These conditions highlighted the risks faced if the facility had shut down entirely because of flooding or a full power loss. Not all of the markets have backup generators, and the electrical vaults

are at street level, barely one or two feet above the cofferdam. Severe damage would have taken weeks to return the facility to full operation. Although Hunts Point escaped the most severe impact of Sandy, it is clearly both critical and vulnerable.

Other risks, in addition to hurricanes, storm surges, and flooding issues, can affect Hunts Point markets. They are also at risk from snowstorms, heat waves, and terrorism. Investing in comprehensive disaster planning for the markets is essential.

preparing it for more intense weather events. But not all infrastructure is of the same critical importance for life and safety. Because the funds for preparing the region for the climate of the future and for general upgrading are limited, regional priorities must be set, making it important to distinguish between infrastructure that must operate with only the briefest of interruptions and infrastructure that can be allowed to fail safely for longer periods.

CRITICAL IN A CRISIS: CASCADING EFFECTS AND UNPREDICTABLE IMPACTS

Costs associated with flood protection and other resiliency measures must be considered comprehensively, taking into account the value of the lives and assets protected and the potential impact on improving the economy and the quality of life. Critical life- and safety-related infrastructure needs to remain functional, though other infrastructure systems may be allowed to fail safely during such crises as extreme temperatures, earthquakes, winds, floods, waves, overuse, and terrorism (physical, digital, and biological). Federal, state, and local governments already prepare for many of these events through emergency and disaster planning. However, myriad cascading effects and varying impacts can be unforeseen and will remain somewhat unpredictable.

Because infrastructure relies heavily on linked networks, damage to one system or even just a component can have cascading effects on the others. For example, a food supply requires transportation, which requires fuel and accessible road-, rail-, and waterways, as well as power for refrigeration and storage. Thus, a fuel shortage not only limits emergency response transportation but also hampers the food supply network. This delicate, interdependent relationship between infrastructure components and networks can cause unpredictable effects. The ever-changing nature of infrastructure systems means that decision makers must be constantly engaged in analyzing and defining these networks to ensure that investments and preparedness plans reinforce resiliency and quick recoveries from disasters.

WHAT ARE CRITICAL SYSTEMS?

Many of our systems function well both every day and in crisis, whereas others are highly vulnerable. The debate as to which components of each infrastructure network are critical to life and safety and how long others can safely be out should continue to be an ongoing public debate, especially as technology and societal demands continue to evolve. This debate needs to occur concurrently with cost/benefit analysis during utility rate cases or infrastructure capital budgeting processes.

Although some elements of a community can survive without power or public transportation for a limited time, access to drinking water, food, shelter, hospitals, and public emergency communication infrastructures are not luxuries—they cannot be offline for more than a few hours. Likewise, elevators in buildings with the old, infirm, or handicapped need to be back online within a few hours of an emergency. These critical emergency infrastructures all need electricity to operate, but that does not dictate that the entire electrical power grid be fully functional during disasters. The accurate

Six weeks after Hurricane Sandy, a Consolidated Edison repair crew works on underground recovery and repairs to the infrastructure along Broad Street in the Financial District of Lower Manhattan.

assessment of critical infrastructures and their vulnerabilities, and recognition of the cascading effects that events can have on these types of networks, form a strategic part of regional planning and preparing for crises. Recognition of alternative technologies (such as battery and microgeneration) and development of backup plans need "precrisis" attention.

The following are some examples of critical infrastructure:

» Emergency communications;

» Critical institutions (hospitals and shelters);

» Emergency response (police, fire, EMTs, leaders, community volunteers);

» Food supply (distribution, access, and storage);

» Fuel supply (distribution, access, and storage);

» Water supply (distribution, access, and storage);

» Buildings that house vulnerable populations (climate control especially in extreme heat or cold weather, elevators, water, communications); and

» Sewage treatment and outflow systems.

RECOMMENDATION 6

DEVELOP A REGIONAL INFRASTRUCTURE VISION, REVIEW IT REGULARLY, AND SET PRIORITIES.

A population's needs and technology frequently change faster than built infrastructure and forecasting models can keep up with. In light of both varying event impacts, and changing needs and technology, analysis and definitions of critical infrastructure are likely to change and must be reviewed frequently and comprehensively.

Infrastructure planning and investment must be guided by a shared vision among the stakeholders and by a systemic framework. In a systemic framework, parts reinforce each other across infrastructure and service sectors that are under the authority of different jurisdictions and often run independently of each other despite their fundamental interconnectedness. It is essential that a vision of a comprehensive infrastructure framework relate to the growing demand and unique physical characteristics of the region as a coherent whole, not as a series of independent parts. Such a vision must be relevant to both dense urban areas and coastal communities.

RECOMMENDATION 7

CONSIDER LONG-TERM RESILIENCY WHEN EVALUATING REBUILDING STRATEGIES.

For many regions, the available financial resources for capital investments fall drastically short of the cost of proposed resiliency and protection projects. Cost/benefit analysis of infrastructure investments is an excellent tool for regional decision makers to employ in comprehensively evaluating the implementation strategies for long-term resiliency. Governments can concentrate public money on protecting major critical public infrastructure as well as encouraging private owners to develop resilient protective measures, but major public infrastructure investment decisions must be supported by a cost/benefit analysis and prioritization criteria.

To select a rational sequence and strategy for implementation of resiliency measures, criteria for prioritization need to be established that include a cost/benefit assessment of the following factors:

1. Criticality of Need

The criticality of need is fundamental. Addressing human safety and extraordinary exposures can outweigh baseline property value considerations. Consideration should be given to (a) the degree to which a given measure mitigates a risk with a higher probability of occurrence (for example, land uses in the lowest elevations are more at risk to future flooding and surge conditions); (b) the urgency of need, such as how important a measure is implemented by a given milestone in time (for example, the introduction of submersible equipment by electric utilities in time for next year's hurricane season); (c) the degree to which a measure mitigates risk to public health and safety; (d) the degree to which a measure mitigates multiple sources of risk (for example, wind, water, surge, snow); and (e) the establishment of multiple layers of risk mitigation that create redundancy across urban systems.

2. Market Value Protected

The economic value of infrastructure, real estate, businesses, and public assets like libraries, parks, and theaters, all of which translate into jobs, is paramount. However, perhaps of equal or close to equal importance, is social and cultural value. Community leaders must decide the value of protecting certain communities and demographics. There must be an assessment of (a) the value of infrastructure and real estate assets to be protected; (b) the adverse impact on property values arising from damage to other urban systems (transportation, utilities, health care, essential supplies—gas, food, water); (c) the economic value to be protected (jobs, workforce capacity, tax revenue); and (d) the social and cultural values to be protected (affordable housing, neighborhood integrity, cultural resources).

Job centers across the region represent areas and districts of concentrated value (value zones) whose resilience needs to be prioritized to ensure that the region's economy can perform in an uninterrupted manner. The costs associated with business interruption are typically as large as or even larger than property damage associated with weather events.

Individual buildings will be subject to new building codes requiring the relocation of heating, ventilation, and air-conditioning equipment from basements to upper floors of existing buildings. These code revisions need to recognize that the economic value of existing leasable building areas will be adversely affected. Strategies and policy frameworks need to be devised to protect owners from losing cash flow from real estate assets through mechanisms such as flexibility in code requirements, such as increasing floor/area ratio to compensate for loss of leasable space and property tax abatement.

3. Potential Market Value to Be Created

An assessment of market potential is vital. The evaluation must incorporate not only new streams of revenue but also the potential to achieve climate mitigation goals or the creation of other cobenefits or public purpose, like open space. The panel recommends that New York City pursue the consideration of Seaport City as a way to create additional

CRITERIA FOR PRIORITIZATION

Criticality of Need	The degree to which a given measure mitigates a risk with a higher probability of occurrence *Example: land uses in the lowest elevations are more at risk to future flooding and surge conditions*
	Urgency of need, that is, how important a measure is implemented by a given milestone in time *Example: the introduction of submersible equipment by electric utilities in time for next year's hurricane season*
	The degree to which a measure mitigates risk to public health and safety
	The degree to which a measure mitigates multiple sources of risk *Example: wind, water, surge, storm*
	Establishment of multiple layers of risk mitigation that create redundancy across urban systems
Market Value Protected	Assessment of value of infrastructure and real estate assets to be protected
	Adverse impact on property values arising from damage to other urban systems *Example: transportation, utilities, health care, essential supplies (gas, food, water)*
	Economic value to be protected *Example: jobs, workforce capacity, tax revenue*
	Social and cultural values to be protected *Example: affordable housing, neighborhood integrity, cultural resources*
Potential Market Value to Be Created	Measures that create new revenue streams or create future value potential
	Measures that achieve climate mitigation goals *Example: energy efficiency*
	Measures that create other cobenefits and achieve other public purposes *Example: open-space creation*
Additional Performance Considerations	Ease of project execution across multijurisdictional permitting authorities
	Opportunity to leverage the existing finance and delivery capacity of existing development entities
	Certainty and availability of funding *Example: timing, probability, complexity of comingled funding*
	Durability and designed life cycle of a given measure
	Operations and maintenance costs
	The degree to which a project is a component of a systematic implementation strategy; demonstration projects to establish political feasibility; projects that advance research and development objectives

development areas and to create a value-capture mechanism to fund the protection system in Lower Manhattan. Seaport City represents a multipurpose strategy for shoreline protection, which also creates new economic value by developing a major urban project. Irrespective of the feasibility of that specific project, this strategy of embracing new waterfront development in certain high-value locations could be executed at a variety of scales across the region and can create the necessary ingredients for effective public/private partnerships that generate new sources of revenue, offer new delivery mechanisms, and establish new buffers for surrounding neighborhoods. Smaller-scale strategies might include the creation of new waterfront parks that introduce new resiliency measures but that also create public amenities, thereby increasing land value for surrounding upland sites. Ample precedents exist for using these kinds of open-space improvements as a component of broader value-capture finance mechanisms.

4. Additional Performance Considerations

Other project criteria that factor into decision making, but that have less impact and are perhaps even ancillary to prioritization, include the typical project evaluation criteria, such as (a) the ease of project execution across multijurisdictional permitting authorities; (b) the ability to leverage existing financing and delivery capacity of existing development entities; (c) the certainty and availability of funding (timing, probability, complexity of comingled funding); (d) the durability and designed life cycle of a given measure; and (e) operations and maintenance costs; among others.

RECOMMENDATION 8

DESIGN PROTECTIVE INFRASTRUCTURE TO DO MORE THAN PROTECT.

Given the significant allocation of public resources to infrastructure created both to improve resiliency and to increase the competitiveness of the region, building protective measures that serve only to protect is far from the best use of limited resources. Protective infrastructure can serve multiple functions. It can be of great economic and ecological value if it is designed in a way that contributes to the creation of new development opportunities, doubles up to accommodate other infrastructure uses, improves the quality of the public realm and waterfront experience, and enhances natural systems. Such strategies for multifunctional protective infrastructure must be site specific and must demand a design that is suitable for coastal communities with delicate natural ecosystems, as well as for high-density urban areas that require efficient use of available space. The private sector can also become a partner to enhance economic viability of flood protection infrastructure by including commercial and residential development in the plan. Combining budgets from multiple funding sources optimizes the deployment of investment.

THE AMSTERDAM CENTRAAL TRAIN STATION

NIK MORRIS (VAN LEIDEN)

Originally built in 1889, the Amsterdam Centraal railway station is one of the main rail hubs in the Netherlands with almost 250,000 travelers daily. Following the recommendations of engineers, the train station is situated north of the city and separates Amsterdam city from the waterfront. Although the placement of the train station was highly criticized by the public at the time for "limiting the beauty of the city" and slowing the city's growth toward the north, the train station additionally functions as a dike, protecting the city's core from floods.

RECOMMENDATION 9

EXPLORE THE POTENTIAL OF SOFT SYSTEMS.

A multifunctional approach to infrastructure can occur through soft and hard design. Soft systems typically refer to embracing the living system and enabling natural systems to efficiently address issues like stormwater management or shoreline protection. Hard systems are engineered solutions that make use of manmade materials and technologies. As the New York–New Jersey region begins to carefully consider its infrastructure network as a tool for resiliency and recovery, it is well positioned to be on the forefront of integrating more soft infrastructure into the overall system. Incorporating soft infrastructure can also be a cost-effective way to build systems that protect the region's 520 miles of coastline.

The coastal protection function of existing shoreline systems can be increased dramatically through new living systems that can be created from scratch by the strategic placement of natural elements, such as plants, stone, sand, and other materials. In addi-tion, these types of living, soft systems often have intrinsic multifunctional capabilities. For example, in many areas of New Jersey and New York, natural systems such as dunes, maritime forests, wetlands, reefs, water storage ponds, creeks, and inlets not only are cost-effective, resilient forms of coastal protection infrastructure, but they also reduce tem-perature; enhance natural resources, water quality, and air quality; and provide public access to the water, improving quality of life.

Natural systems address environmental and protection concerns naturally, whereas hard systems are too often one-purpose solutions that may require significantly more investment. For example, break-waters and reefs cause storm surge waves to break off shore before they reach land, and dunes absorb wave energy. Hard protection systems, on the other hand, like seawalls and levees, are only truly effective in sealing out water when they are long and unbroken, requiring a massive infrastructure investment. A strong infrastructure system is best achieved through the use of both hard and soft elements. Creating an

SEAPORT CITY

In December 2012, Mayor Michael Bloomberg created the Special Initiative for Rebuilding and Resiliency (SIRR) to address creating a more resilient New York City in the wake of Hurricane Sandy, with a long-term focus on preparing for and protecting against the impacts of climate change. The initiative's report *PlaNYC: A Stronger, More Resilient New York* (released in June 2013) provides more than 250 actionable recommen-dations both for rebuilding the communities affected by Sandy and for increasing the resilience of infrastructure and buildings citywide. The recommendations are based on the central principles that initiatives for resiliency should be ambitious but achievable, should stretch resources to maximize benefits per dollar, and should protect, not aban-don, coastal neighborhoods. In addition, the strategies recommended in this report hold a multilayered approach, seeking to build coastal defenses, to design new and retrofit existing buildings for resiliency, and to protect critical city infrastructure and services.

This summer, the mayor's office issued a request for proposals to conduct studies for the feasibility of devel-oping a multipurpose levee (MPL) along the eastern edge of Lower Manhattan in the East River. The MPL would shield 1.5 miles of coast, which remain vulnerable to fu-ture events. The levee would be constructed to enable the building of residential and commercial developments on top of it. The proposed de-velopment, known as Seaport City, is intended to be an inte-gral part of a comprehensive shield for Lower Manhattan.

Multipurpose levees func-tion much like a simple levee, but they play additional roles, for example, serving as transportation infrastructure; providing parking; supporting residential, retail, or commer-cial uses; or serving as open space. In certain high-den-sity locations, multipurpose levees not only can serve as flood protection for adjacent neighborhoods but also can provide a cost-effective mechanism to pay for coastal protection by creating land for development, which is also elevated and thus itself not at risk of flooding.

Source: NYC Special Initiative for Rebuilding and Resiliency, *PlaNYC: A Stronger, More Resilient New York*, 2013, p. 56, http://www.nyc.gov/html/sirr/html/report/report.shtml.

effective mix of hard and soft infrastructure, however, will require innovation in soft systems and a commitment of resources and expertise similar to that given to hard infrastructure. The resulting system, however, may be far more cost-effective; high-tech natural systems can be combined with hard systems to reduce total investment cost and effectiveness. For example, a mix of structure and plants combined with hard infrastructure like bulkheads and seawalls

can reduce the height and cost of the seawalls. Modeling shows that for particular stretches of shoreline, the height of a seawall or dune can be reduced by one to two feet for every mile of wetland.

RECOMMENDATION 10

ALLOW FOR SAFE FAILURE OF SOME NONCRITICAL INFRASTRUCTURE SYSTEMS.

At times, infrastructure networks will be down. Generating awareness of this fact and setting regulations as well as public expectations of reasonable levels of service and the likelihood of service interruptions will prevent loss of life and minimize loss of property and are crucial to resilient infrastructure planning. Adaptation and learning from past mistakes can often offer important advances in strategy, but there is no avoiding infrastructure disruption, even in regions as strong as the New York–New Jersey area. The temporary failure of those systems that are not critical for life and safety should be anticipated and planned for. New York City subway lines are delayed all the time, and occasionally the power goes out and cell phone towers go down; at some point, all networks experience failures.

RECOMMENDATION 11

CREATE INFRASTRUCTURE RECOVERY PLANS FOR QUICK PARTIAL SERVICE RESTORATION.

Despite the resilient "bounce back" attitude of most communities during and after extreme events, as was the case with Hurricane Sandy, many citizens experienced infrastructure outages that exceeded acceptable standards, even considering the extreme nature of the storm.

In the days following a major disaster, the speed at which a region's infrastructure system returns to partial operation dictates the degree to which the disaster affects the region's economy and the livelihoods of people in harm's way. Priorities for restoration should be set by stakeholders, and the infrastructure system should be, to the extent possible, designed to accommodate those priorities quickly in the wake of a disaster. This objective could be approached through stages of restoration that focus on bringing power back to high-priority infrastructure components, such as gas stations or grocery

ROCKAWAYS: THE ARVERNE EAST PROJECT

In 2007, a consortium of three developers announced plans for "Arverne East," a 47-acre site in the Rockaways that had been left fallow since the Arverne Urban Renewal Project removed thousands of summer bungalows and stores over 35 years ago. But the new proposal stalled in the struggling economy. The subsequent damage brought by the storm to most of the area, along with the fact that an adjacent development designed to meet major storms and flooding—Arverne by the Sea—avoided significant harm, reinvigorated the need to look for resilient recovery alternatives through collaboration and community engagement. Existing dunes and vegetation in combination with the boardwalk structure absorbed a substantial amount of the Sandy storm surge. This, in combination with Arverne East's newly installed stormwater management system and the additional vertical height requirement above the base flood elevation, provided a layered system of protection from flooding.

The Arverne East design competition, announced in June

2013, is an example of how new resiliency design criteria are being incorporated into community planning in coastal communities of New York City. The project, on an 80-acre site in the Rockaways, is a collaboration among the New York City Department of Housing Preservation and Development (NYC HPD), a consortium of developers who won a 2007 competition, and two local community groups to revitalize an oceanfront parcel, the still-vacant urban renewal clearance site.

The open ideas competition attracted over 100 entries that explored a wide variety of solutions for flood protection and community development. The project combines private sector mixed-use development investment with public sector funding for a seawall that creates an integrated public park, which provides a neighborhood-wide public amenity, as well as a flood protection feature. The oceanfront property under consideration has the potential to be a laboratory for possible solutions for the future of coastal development in the city and several other areas around the country.

stores. In regions that rely on it, public transportation should also be restored with minimal service or stopgap measures. Continued distributions of food staples and water are essential and should be a top priority for restoration if they are interrupted. These types of needs could be broken down into individual subsystems that are able to function independently for short periods so that small components of systems can operate while the wider network is down.

RECOMMENDATION 12

ENCOURAGE INDIVIDUAL PREPAREDNESS DURING SHORT-TERM INFRASTRUCTURE OUTAGES.

Those in areas at risk for power outage, transportation limitation, or property damage should be ready for a wide range of system disruptions in the case of a climate event. The public should not presume that infrastructure systems will operate perfectly post-disaster. When power outages or other operational failures are predicted, citizens should be empowered to take individual responsibility for preparing for the likely scale and effects of the event. Such preparation will require reliable, frequent, and timely distribution of information by the public sector. Communication and leadership in the proliferation of information and education of citizens are critical components of this individual preparedness.

Historically, social networks and community-based organizations (CBOs) have been the most successful providers of immediate relief after a disaster and could also be a secondary source of ongoing relief. To be a secondary source, these organizations must be prepared with goods to support the needs during power outages and other interruptions. Even private sector building managers and owners have a role and responsibility to prepare themselves and their tenants for days without noncritical infrastructure systems; it is good practice and ultimately better for the bottom line. The next step for many building owners would be to create redundancies within the system by installing generators for the elevators or emergency power in the case of power failure. As shown during Sandy, the New York City Housing Authority had failed to invest in generators for its housing, and many individuals were stranded on the upper floors of high-rise public housing projects.

DATA-DRIVEN SUCCESS IN EMERGENCY MANAGEMENT: PALANTIR

Palantir recently coordinated with Team Rubicon (a disaster-response organization) in response to Hurricane Sandy. Palantir is an organization of analysts that develops powerful data management software—used by the Defense Department, Central Intelligence Agency, Federal Bureau of Investigation, U.S. Army, U.S. Marine Corps, U.S. Air Force, New York Police Department, and Los Angeles Police Department—to address logistics problems, common issues for dispatch and relief crews. Team Rubicon made effective use of a Web app created by Palantir for mobile devices to more efficiently mobilize resources and supplies to target areas. Volunteers were able to access data sources (including information on fuel availability, power grids, and medical clinics) and could more readily be repositioned to areas of highest demand. Using real-time data collected on the ground with Palantir software, Team Rubicon was able to collect, centralize, and assess requests for assistance according to urgency, thus streamlining the relief process. This process not only improved the quality and currency of information but also drastically aided in the sharing of information, not only with the federal, state, and local governments but also with individuals and communities, thus better informing them for rebuilding and recovery decision making.

AFTER SANDY: ADVANCING STRATEGIES FOR LONG-TERM RESILIENCE AND ADAPTABILITY

Finance, Investment, and Insurance

The property markets are accustomed to taking into account a broad range of market risk factors that are reflected in the pricing of debt and equity investments and insurance rates for residential and commercial real estate. In the northeastern United States, one of the more recent issues that property owners, lenders, and insurers have had to consider is the exposure of assets located in flood zones to casualty losses resulting from the unprecedented rise in sea levels associated with extreme weather conditions, such as Hurricane Sandy. This exposure is forcing coastal communities across the region to rethink the ways in which their land is used.

Many communities are facing the politically challenging task of balancing the natural human desire to restore and continue existing land uses for homes and businesses on the one hand with the often dramatic increases in the costs of protecting and rebuilding those structures most at risk on the other. As this tension is played out with a growing understanding of the long-term implications of climate change and sea level rise, new policies, investment strategies, and land uses will evolve.

Market participants and government agencies are developing a greater understanding of the new risks associated with real estate located in expanding flood zones, which themselves are being redefined

THIS PAGE, FROM LEFT: OFFICIAL WHITE HOUSE PHOTO/PETE SOUZA; METROPOLITAN TRANSPORTATION AUTHORITY/PATRICK CASHIN; ULI; DEMERZEL21. FACING PAGE, FROM TOP: LEONARD ZHUKOVSKY; SPIRITARTIST based on updated climatological data and FEMA maps.

FEMA has recently issued new flood zone maps, and Congress has recently passed new legislation regarding the administration of the National Flood Insurance Program. Planning and building departments of local municipalities are in the early stages of formulating zoning and building codes to take into account the new flood zones and FEMA standards. Thus, a significant amount of uncertainty exists among property owners affected by Sandy as to whether and how to rebuild their properties; what the cost will be to rebuild based on the new standards; whether financing or insurance proceeds will be available to pay for the cost of rebuilding; and whether coverage will be available in sufficient amounts for future flood insurance. Similarly, some jurisdictions like New York City are creating or changing their own evacuation zones, compounding the uncertainty for local landowners, lenders, and others.

City, state, and federal agencies have identified a broad range of infrastructure projects that, if implemented, could improve coastal communities' ability to withstand future extreme weather conditions and reduce the exposure of properties in nearby flood zones to damage or destruction. New York City's alone calls for $14 billion in infrastructure investment over a ten-year period. It is completely unknown at this time which if any of these protections will be implemented, and when. This indetermination only adds to the uncertainty of landowners and others.

Property markets are accustomed to taking into account a broad range of market risk factors that are reflected in the pricing of debt and equity investment and insurance rates for residential and commercial real estate. But the current confusion is making this repricing uncertain. As the growing weather-related risks become better understood and priced into the markets, it will force reconsideration of current and future land prices, forcing the reconsideration of land uses, regardless of the desires of residents or government policies.

It is in this context that individual property owners, real estate lenders and insurers, public agencies, and legislatures are confronted with a number of critical issues related to the availability of capital and insurance for improvements located in the newly defined flood zones:

» How should these properties be valued?

» How much will the cost increment be to rebuild to the new FEMA standards?

» Will building codes be amended in all local jurisdictions to meet these standards?

» Will property insurance be available and in sufficient amounts to rebuild, and how should flood insurance be priced?

» Where should coastal storm protective infrastructure improvements (such as dunes, bulkheads, floodgates, and revetments) be made, how might they be paid for, and how will these improvements affect nearby properties' flood exposure?

» Can supplemental funding sources be accessed on a state or regional basis to improve storm emergency preparedness and management programs?

» What role should the private sector and industry leaders such as the Urban Land Institute play in recovery and preparedness efforts?

In this section, the panel offers recommendations regarding these issues and how best to address them. Though not comprehensive, these recommendations shed light on major reform and policy changes that need to be addressed in light of a changing climate.

SOURCES OF FINANCE

Capital is the lifeblood of infrastructure and real estate development and rebuilding. Without sufficient funds, it is impossible to make the improvements necessary to prepare for future extreme weather events and to rebuild in the aftermath of Hurricane Sandy.

RECOMMENDATION 13

IMPLEMENT CREATIVE EXTRAMUNICIPAL FINANCING MECHANISMS.

Because of the magnitude of capital requirements and the frequently extramunicipal scope of many infrastructure improvements, these projects can only be undertaken by federal or state agencies in cooperation with local municipalities or through a regional authority empowered to raise capital based on the state's credit rating. At the present time, there is a gap in funding sources for resiliency infrastructure projects. So it is incumbent on states to coordinate and create their own resiliency funding authorities. In the case of New York and New Jersey, a new funding authority could be created. But agencies such as the Port Authority of New York and New Jersey also already exist that could work with federal authorities to design and fund resilience infrastructure improvements.

Another area of resiliency preparedness that lends itself to extramunicipal financing is the need to create state- and region-wide emergency management programs that can build the capacity of individual municipalities and public and private support organizations to prepare for and recover from extreme weather. Many smaller towns and communities do not have the resources to invest in resiliency planning and recovery programs on their own.

RECOMMENDATION 14

REVISE FEDERAL FUNDING ASSISTANCE TO ALLOW LOCAL DISCRETION AND DIRECT FUNDING FLOWS TO COMMUNITIES WHEN POSSIBLE.

Storm recovery money from the federal government comes with specific uses attached that limit the flexibility of towns and cities in spending to improve multiple infrastructures simultaneously. Frequently, federal assistance funds singular, single-use projects. For example, Army Corps of Engineers money cannot be used to design or build public realm elements like a bikeway on top of a seawall, or flood protection softscapes designed to maximize habitat and public use. There are too many nondiscretionary resources and too few human resources to integrate them effectively in this manner. If such federal assistance were more flexible, infrastructure investments would be more powerful and would more effectively serve the communities in which they are made.

More flexibility in federal or state spending programs would allow communities to establish their own context-specific standards for a layered, multiscalar infrastructure system. Such flexibility would allow a context-sensitive approach that meets the needs of individual communities. So, for example, instead of the individual's being required to raise a house 12 feet or the community's building a massive 16-foot seawall, both of which will have a deleterious effect on quality of life, funding could support a multiscalar effort to change community standards to raise houses three feet, speed neighborhood drainage with the addition of bioswales, raise the coastal edge five feet with a terraced public space, or deepen freshwater creeks and ponds by five feet to reduce back-flooding.

RECOMMENDATION 15

PROVIDE SMALL COMMUNITIES WITH FINANCIAL SUPPORT TO REPLACE LOST LOCAL TAX DOLLARS.

Although Sandy devastated individual neighborhoods within New York City and caused significant short-term economic disruptions, the long-term impact on the city's municipal finances will be relatively limited. By contrast, municipalities with fewer resources that experienced more concentrated damage have experienced significant short-term strain, and their long-term financial viability has been threatened. One underappreciated consequence of municipal fragmentation is that it results in a large number of small communities, many of which will have more than 50 percent of their homes and businesses damaged.

In the immediate aftermath of the disaster, municipalities incurred numerous unplanned-for

FLORIDA EMERGENCY MANAGEMENT, PREPAREDNESS, AND ASSISTANCE

As a result of its exposure to multiple Category 3–5 hurricanes in a given year, the state of Florida has established an innovative program that could be applicable to the Northeast and other regions. The Florida legislature created a $2–$4 surcharge on the premiums of all property, flood, and wind insurance policies, the proceeds of which are deposited directly in the state's Emergency Management, Preparedness, and Assistance Trust Fund. This fund is used only to establish emergency preparedness plans and tools that are shared with all counties and cities in Florida, as well as with the Board of Tourism and the Chamber of Commerce. The product of this program is a resilient communications network and set of emergency management protocols that permit public and private stakeholders to minimize the impact of hurricanes and to recover more quickly.

expenditures on items like demolition and emergency relief and have exhausted what little surpluses they may have had to manage these items. This is often exacerbated by opaque rules from FEMA on what items are eligible for reimbursement. For example, there is no clear policy on whether FEMA will pay to regrade, fill, or seed sites that have been demolished.

In the medium term, property assessments will drop because of storm damage, and this drop can even extend to undamaged properties in the municipality. Although towns can make up for the drop in assessments by increasing the millage rates (a property tax rate expressed in tenths of a cent that is applied to the assessed value of real estate), there will be dislocations as those whose values (and therefore assessments) have not been reduced find that their total tax bill has increased by the increased millage rates. These effects have still not yet

been felt by the communities given the time delays in assessing properties and billing at these new, lowered valuations.

Finally, over the long term, as families struggle to rebuild and grapple with rising insurance rates, property values can permanently decline, and blighted properties may begin to emerge, especially in communities where the cost of meeting minimum code and elevation requirements exceeds the market value of a property. The risk to property assessments also makes it nearly impossible for small municipalities to consider restricting rebuilding or restricting future development since that would create an existential threat to their tax base.

The panel recommends that consideration be given to a state disaster mechanism to offset the loss of property taxes in communities that restrict redevelopment of sites where properties have been destroyed and instead dedicate the land to public purposes, such as natural infrastructure. As part of this proposed program, the panel believes that any turnover of land that is offset in this way should be deeded for public use in perpetuity.

The state should consider offsetting taxes formerly generated from properties that a municipality chooses to eliminate development upon, particularly when such land can be used for natural infrastructure or to provide public access to beaches. Since most municipalities are dependent on local property taxes, it can be next to impossible for them to prevent rebuilding or generally impede development without threatening their existence, therefore a tax offset would be particularly important.

RECOMMENDATION 16

ACCURATELY PRICE CLIMATE RISK INTO PROPERTY VALUE AND INSURANCE.

Insurance programs have an enormous impact on both existing buildings and new construction. Insurance affects many aspects of the real estate market: the availability and often the amount of mortgage financing; the long-term viability of investments; the market assessment of acceptable risks by owners, lenders, tenants, and other stakeholders; and, indirectly, the implicit public policies that guide market investment and disinvestment decisions. These components operate in a wide variety of contexts, and the analysis differs for office buildings in Lower Manhattan versus single-family homes on the New Jersey or Long Island shores versus public housing in Coney Island. Climate risk is a comparatively new challenge for the insurance world, and we need to enhance analysis and public understanding in this arena.

The availability of equity and debt capital is strongly affected by insurance. In 1968, Congress created the National Flood Insurance Program, which enabled property owners in participating communities to purchase flood insurance. Under federal law, the purchase of flood insurance is mandatory for all lenders that are federally licensed or regulated (that is, banks and credit unions) for the acquisition or construction of buildings in high-risk flood areas (Special Flood Hazard Areas, or SFHAs). This requirement includes all loans made, purchased, or guaranteed by Fannie Mae, Freddie Mac, or the Department of Housing and Urban Development. The net effect is that all but privately held mortgages require flood insurance on properties in flood areas. The required insurance amounts are set by FEMA with a cap of $250,000 on structures. Until the Biggert-Waters bill was passed in 2012, premiums were not claims based, and an estimated 1.12 million or 20 percent of the 5.6 million NFIP policies in force were subsidized with rates as low as $553 per year. Under Biggert-Waters, subsidized policyholders on nonprimary residences or businesses in flood areas will see premiums rise 25 percent per year until full risk rates are achieved. Effective October 1, 2013, premiums for new or lapsed policies will be at full risk rates, which in certain high-risk coastal areas could exceed $20,000, again with a $250,000 cap.

Under the law, flood maps, many dating back to the 1970s and 1980s, are now being updated. Drafts have been issued and are being finalized. FEMA hasn't estimated the number of structures that will be located in the new SFHAs. However, in late 2014, if the timeline is followed, all property owners—including those not currently subsidized but as a result of the new SFHA maps are now in a flood zone—will see premium increases of 20 percent per year to reach full risk rates.

These changes will increase the cost of occupying mortgaged properties in SFHAs and have already affected value as any new owner will be paying the full risk premium. These are annual policies; premiums are not capped.

Insurance markets cover a range of risks and are provided under private and publicly regulated programs. For example, FEMA flood insurance operates with a different set of rules and incentives than the limited market in private flood insurance. Casualty, business interruption, wind, and other types of coverage each have their own specific requirements. Market-based risk pricing should be the starting point for flood zone financing and insurance programs and can be modified for public policy purposes.

» **Risk must be priced accurately.** Although this is a truism for insurance, it appears that much more study and information are required, especially with respect to flood insurance. Scientific and engineering understanding of flood risk is rapidly evolving, in part due to new experiences, such as Hurricane Sandy. In addition, FEMA programs have been strongly influenced by political considerations and often contentious debate.

» **Insurance pricing should be examined to determine whether market distortions are occurring because of misunderstanding of climatic events.** In certain areas outside the New York–New Jersey region, it appears that insurance premiums have increased in response to climate events, even for types of insurance coverage that are not tied directly to the impact of such events. For example, basic casualty insurance typically excludes flood and wind coverage.

» **Despite the view that government assistance programs distort the market and often encourage unwise rebuilding and new development,** certain insurance markets still require these programs as a form of backstop. For example, presently, the state of New Jersey and the federal government pay for more than 90 percent of sand replenishment along the shore, and until recently the NFIP has provided significant subsidies to coastal living.

RECOMMENDATION 17

ALLOW PARTIAL COMPLIANCE AND MITIGATION MEASURES IN ORDER TO CREATE FLEXIBILITY IN INSURANCE PREMIUMS.

To obtain mortgage financing in a flood zone hazard area, one must qualify for FEMA insurance (which has a $250,000 insured coverage limit). In turn, to obtain FEMA insurance, a property must adhere to newly established flood zone building standards. In the case of new construction, this requirement may not be an issue (except for the higher cost of construction to meet these building elevation and design standards). However, older buildings may be able to comply partially with these requirements but not completely. For example, a building owner may be able to relocate mechanical equipment above flood levels, but it may be impossible or prohibitively expensive to raise the elevation of the building (or for that matter a violation of applicable zoning). Thus, one way to facilitate the rebuilding and recovery process for lower-income households and small businesses would be for FEMA to permit

partial compliance with flood zone building requirements in order to qualify for its insurance, perhaps at a lower amount or with a premium surcharge to reflect the increased casualty risk.

» **Insurance pricing needs to more accurately reflect risk assessment based on mitigation.** For example, flood insurance premiums will of course be reduced if a home is raised above the BFE (base flood elevation). However, appropriate reductions should also be considered (which may be smaller) in flood mitigation programs where some but not all measures have been employed, for example, if the home is below the BFE but mechanical systems have either been flood-proofed or raised above the BFE. Similarly, raising dunes or constructing other flood protection measures should arguably lead to reduced premiums, even without home improvements. In the same vein, compliance with upgraded building codes should lead to reduced premiums. Such mitigation measures may be appropriate under circumstances in which it is impossible or prohibitively expensive to raise the elevation of the building.

» **Integrating careful assessment of the value of flood mitigation efforts should also encourage investment in retrofits,** which can reduce the impact (cost, duration, displacement) of future extreme climate events and thereby protect major private market investments, for example, the Lower Manhattan office market, which obviously suffered during Sandy.

RECOMMENDATION 18

DESIGN FINANCING TO HELP RELIEVE THE RECOVERY BURDEN FOR LOW-INCOME HOUSEHOLDS AND SMALL BUSINESSES.

At the homeowner and small-business level, the ability to obtain financing to rebuild as soon as possible following a major storm, and to do so in accordance with the latest FEMA regulations and local building codes, is an essential part of creating resilient communities. For higher-income property owners with personal resources and private insurance, rebuilding is often not a problem. However, lower-income households and small businesses without substantial savings are disadvantaged.

To finance or relieve some of this burden, federal, state, and local authorities might consider a number of possible financing mechanisms. It is vital, however, that subsidies and tax abatements do not distort individuals' or businesses' decision-making processes on whether or how to rebuild in certain areas. Although the panel explicitly recognizes the ability of individuals and communities to rebuild, it does not mean their choice should necessarily be subsidized. Any subsidies or tax abatements provided by the government should be strategically targeted to designated value zones or other locations where rebuilding is a priority.

Should a covered climate event result in a settlement, these funds could be used to repair the damage, but they may fall below the cost of repairs, especially if building to new codes (elevating the structure) in the most vulnerable areas. For those without other personal financial resources, a new state program could be created, similar to a Green Acres Program, which, through an allocation of sales tax receipts or by broadening the authority of existing funds, could provide an alternative to homeowners. Based on a valuation formula, funds could be lent to the homeowner from the fund.

There would be two options for repayment: (a) funds could be repaid by the titled owner from his or her own sources over a limited time (not through a sale or transfer) and returned to the fund for reuse, or (b) a "life estate" could be created whereby the homeowner had use of the property until death or destruction by a climate event. In this case, title would pass to the state, essentially resulting in the delayed purchase of the property under the Green Acres fund. Over time, this program could offer a way for sensitive or vulnerable lands to be redirected into conservation and mitigation programs and public use.

Another source of funds that could be used is an assessment on all homeowners' existing insurance policies. Collected by the insurance carrier through the payment process and remitted to the state, these funds could be used for climate mitigation activities or relief purposes. They could also be used to help soften the effects of future increases in the NFIP premiums for those in vulnerable areas.

Other initiatives that might be considered by policy makers and lenders that could facilitate recovery efforts would be temporary property tax abatements and supplemental state-sponsored financing programs that have more flexibility than FEMA and could be targeted to certain areas or circumstances.

» **In certain circumstances, it may be appropriate to establish programs that phase in insurance market pricing over time or that create other financial devices that cushion the blow of increased costs.** Political decision makers may conclude that certain market sectors, neighborhoods, or building types cannot feasibly bear the true market cost of flood insurance and other climate-related coverage.

» **Significant uncertainty, lack of information, misunderstanding, and lack of clarity exist about how these insurance markets operate,** in addition to many controversies about whether the current rules, coverage, and priorities make sense from a public policy perspective. Enhancing "insurance literacy," especially in the context of homeowners and property investors obtaining mortgage loans, could yield significant benefits.

THE TERRORISM RISK INSURANCE ACT MODEL

Becoming law on November 26, 2002, the Terrorism Risk Insurance Act (TRIA) was created to fill the severe market shortage for terrorism insurance after September 11, 2001. This federal "backstop" for insurance claims provides reinsurance coverage to insurers in the event of a certified terrorist act. TRIA requires insurers to provide terrorism insurance coverage to their policyholders; however, it is not mandatory for the insured to purchase the coverage except for workers' compensation that is defined by state statutes. This precedent for terrorism insurance and cooperation among the insurance, financial, and real estate industries, as well as government policy, may provide a useful lesson for how to approach reforms in flood insurance programs.

TOP: President Barack Obama was greeted by residents asking for help during his visit to areas devastated by Hurricane Sandy. **BOTTOM:** New York City Mayor Michael Bloomberg, appearing shaken by the devastation, tours Breezy Point the day after the hurricane hit.

AFTER SANDY: ADVANCING STRATEGIES FOR LONG-TERM RESILIENCE AND ADAPTABILITY

Leadership and Governance

All American Red Cross
Disaster Assistance Is Free

Government is the structure that allows good leadership to flourish, and good leadership provides the guidance and willingness to make difficult decisions. Although many regional decisions were appropriate in the immediate aftermath of Hurricane Sandy, it is clear, almost one year later, that significant shortcomings remain in the structure and functioning of governance, both as to continuing repair of the damage from Sandy and, more important, in preparing for future similar events both in New York City and New Jersey and in other vulnerable regions.

Long Island and New Jersey are characterized by profound municipal fragmentation. New Jersey alone has more than 550 separate municipalities, over 120 of which have coastal exposures. Such fragmentation is common in many regions along the East Coast. Therefore, careful attention must be paid to the balance between high-level decision making that requires coordination among different levels of government and the need to allow localities the autonomy to make context-sensitive decisions for their communities. For this balance to emerge, all projects' leaders need to come together with urgency and to agree on a list of priorities within the available resources.

THIS PAGE, FROM LEFT: ULI; GYSGT. MICHAEL KROPIEWNICKI; ANTON OPARIN; OFFICIAL WHITE HOUSE PHOTO/PETE SOUZA. FACING PAGE, FROM TOP: OFFICIAL WHITE HOUSE PHOTO/PETE SOUZA; AFP/GETTY IMAGES

RECOMMENDATION 19

DEVOLVE FUNDING TO THE LOWEST EFFECTIVE LEVEL WHERE APPROPRIATE.

Resources should be devolved to the lowest level of government—such as village, township, or city—that can demonstrate capacity to both manage and implement these funds and to coordinate decision making within the region. In the instance of large cities like New York or Jersey City, the criteria for direct funding would likely be met right away with little need for state intermediation, if at all. New York City has nearly the same population as the state of New Jersey and is governed by a single executive with access to considerable resources. New York City's inherent capacity is further augmented by Mayor Bloomberg's strong history of leadership and his freedom to look at the long term. However, the approaching end of his mayoralty raises the question of what approach a new administration will take to preparing the city. Not surprisingly, New York City has created the region's most detailed and thorough plan for long-term response. New York City is also aided by the inherent value of its land and high-density development patterns, which allow it to justify expensive protection measures and infrastructure investments. In some cases, the high land values allow it to shift some or all of these burdens to private developers rather than to rely exclusively on federal funds.

Smaller jurisdictions will likely need to cluster with similarly situated jurisdictions and to develop appropriate infrastructure plans in coordination with the regional entity. Unfortunately, the local political imperative in smaller localities is almost exclusively to help damaged constituents rebuild just as they were before, and there is little room for discussing strategies for mitigation or relocation.

However, although municipal fragmentation limits formal political and governance capacity, it appears to boost the sense of community and allow for a single-minded focus that is valuable in the immediate aftermath of a disaster. The panel was struck by the resourcefulness of the affected municipalities and their ability to identify and often address unmet needs through unconventional channels. As one example, New Jersey's Union Beach transformed its city administrator into a liaison/project manager to assist residents trying to navigate insurance and mortgage processes. Residents of these smaller jurisdictions had a far greater affinity for their local leadership and did not share the same frustration as the residents of New York City's most affected neighborhoods (such as Staten Island and the Rockaways).

RECOMMENDATION 20

ENHANCE THE CAPACITY FOR COORDINATION AND COLLABORATION AMONG DIFFERENT LEVELS OF GOVERNMENT—FROM LOCAL TO FEDERAL.

An inevitable consequence of municipal fragmentation is that many smaller jurisdictions will have limited, if any, emergency response planning capacity or financial reserves for funding repairs and reconstruction. Even fewer of these communities will have experience navigating the labyrinth of rules applicable to federal disaster relief. As such, they are largely at the mercy of the federal bureaucracy and state governments in using these resources. Many of them have part-time mayors, a limited or nonexistent planning staff, volunteer council members, and so forth, who, although dedicated to their communities, simply do not have the expertise or bandwidth to navigate the many layers of government.

To boost the capacity of smaller localities and to promote cooperation among diverse localities while preserving the autonomy and character of the latter, the panel recommends that the federal and state governments provide clear incentives to encourage cooperation among neighboring localities to create local planning clusters. The panel does not envision that either the federal or state governments would dictate these clusters but rather believes that the possibility of local control of federal and state resources will be a carrot sufficient to encourage cooperation. Where it does not happen, power and funds will remain at the state. FEMA (or another federal agency) should fund these planning consortiums for three years. FEMA should have the necessary funds and expertise to assist the towns in outlining clear choices for their long-term resiliency. This assistance would include bringing together NOAA sea level maps, building code requirements, and other relevant studies that show potential long-term conditions for the community.

A search and rescue team arrives at Rockaway Beach Boulevard.

RECOMMENDATION 21

BUILD CAPACITY FOR DECISION MAKING AT THE LOCAL LEVEL.

Localities should be empowered through training and capacity building. Many localities lack capacity and need greater access to information and resources, as well as the support of coordinating entities at higher levels of government. Resources and expertise from other levels of government must have greater duration and continuity than they do currently. Information systems and sharing agreements among coastal communities are needed and can be facilitated by or encouraged by a federal or regional coordinating body. The panel also recommends that the federal government institute, and make permanent, a series of training sessions for local governments to teach them how to prepare for and respond to disasters. These sessions should include both elected officials and key staff.

The panel noted that local elected officials and civic leaders in many of the smaller coastal communities and neighborhoods lacked basic information. If they were more knowledgeable, they would be the best source of information for their constituencies. Besides the hiring of needed staff, the panel believes that a focused program needs to be established immediately to provide training and education about the choices that communities and individuals face. Once people have recovered from the immediate aftermath of the disaster and commenced the longer-term rebuilding, reliable information is necessary to make good long-term decisions. Having people in the community who are trained to provide assistance in making these decisions is also critical.

The role of strong leadership at the local level cannot be ignored. Throughout the Jersey Shore, the

KEVIN DOWNS

45

panel saw significant differences between communities, like Sea Bright, that were willing to explore creative solutions and gather necessary resources and other communities that were primarily concerned with rebuilding the past as quickly as possible. Likewise, Staten Island has an exacerbated sense of exclusion from the decision-making process.

RECOMMENDATION 22

CREATE PROGRAMS TO PROVIDE KNOWLEDGE SHARING AND PROFESSIONAL TRAINING.

As communities start to rebuild and plan for a resilient future, climate change is a factor that must be incorporated into education, training, and professional practices. The entire professional spectrum of advisers that communities and individuals rely on for professional services—including architects, engineers, planners, design professionals, surveyors, and appraisers, as well as investment professionals who contribute to the underlying analysis of investment decisions—must be technically expert in areas that will be integral to decision making and implementation of both mitigation and resilient strategies and practices.

Members of professional organizations must understand the mechanics of how building codes function and interact with other regulations and practices. Appraisers need to have specific expertise about asset classes and practices within the geographic areas in which they work. Underwriters and analysts need to factor climate change into the models they develop and populate. Architects, planners, and designers need to have specific knowledge about incorporating hazard mitigation and climate change into their work and principles.

Education programming examples:

» Professional licensing organizations adopt new standards incorporating mitigation, resilience, and climate change practices into their professional requirements for certification and licensing, including continuing-education requirements.

» Universities incorporate climate change implications into curricula for professional degree programs.

» ULI and other real estate nonprofit educational organizations include course work on climate change practices within their offerings to members and others.

RECOMMENDATION 23

MAKE CRITICAL INFORMATION EASILY UNDERSTANDABLE AND READILY ACCESSIBLE BOTH DURING AND AFTER A DISASTER.

The panel saw a distinct sense among affected communities that they were not receiving adequate or consistent information for making decisions. Most notable was a sense of uncertainty about FEMA base flood elevations (BFEs) and their eventual impact on insurance rates. Communication was and continues to be an issue that could impede the Sandy recovery effort, in particular, and recovery efforts for other disasters, generally. Local governments should be encouraged to use social media and technology to better connect with and inform their constituents about specific recovery efforts.

In addition, leadership should implement an aggressive communication campaign using social media and other outlets to inform and update the public about rising sea levels and associated climate change. Open communications will enhance the capacity of community groups to participate with government and civic leaders to lessen the resistance of the neighborhoods to the effects of climate change and sea level rise. This campaign should incorporate information on elevation, sea level, and related issues into elementary or secondary school materials so teachers understand the risks associated with the school building's location.

Communities must be given the information necessary to learn from the mistakes made during their responses to Hurricane Sandy. Mistakes were as large as not shutting down low-lying power plants in advance of the storm and as small as not providing citizens a list of useful emergency supplies they should purchase and have in their homes. After the storm, instances of misinformation about how to apply for FEMA reimbursement and how to negotiate with insurance companies have led to heart-wrenching tales of people with the full intent of rebuilding to more resilient standards (such as raising the house above the predicted sea level) still not living in their homes.

The latest climate, weather, and flood data need to be publicly available in simple and understandable formats that can be tailored to best reach different audiences within a community, including individual homeowners, renters, and business owners. A program of this nature should also include training and guidance on how to interpret and use the data to inform decision making. It can be challenging to help individuals think about the future in an informed manner. Meeting this challenge requires a great deal of education, information, and, most important, the willingness to lead.

The politics of difficult decisions can paralyze a community, or it can create the collective will to change. The ability to provide a series of grounded facts, and to create a climate in which discussion of those facts and their consequences can take place, enhances the probability of change. The long-term resiliency of the coast depends on hundreds of thousands of individual decisions by property owners—some in beach communities and some in urban neighborhoods. The quality of those decisions in large part will depend on good information. To make informed decisions, people need such critical information as base flood elevations, availability of funding, the cost of insurance, the availability of buyouts, building codes that will be required in flood areas, and the NOAA maps of projected sea level rise—all of which are not easily understood or attainable by individuals.

In each affected community in a region, FEMA (or another federal agency) should allocate funds to hire a community resources person for at least three years postevent to assist the community and its residents. One role will be as an advocate for local residents to clarify choices, to assist in understanding the various financing programs available for rebuilding, and to understand the requirements to rebuild. Another role will be to assist the town in understanding its choices for long-term resiliency.

Two days after the storm hit, President Barack Obama and New Jersey Governor Chris Christie talk with people recovering from Hurricane Sandy while surveying storm damage in Brigantine, New Jersey.

47

Conclusion

The work of this ULI Advisory Services panel is finished, but the work of preparing regions around the United States and the world for the continuing unpredictable impact of climate change and sea level rise will go on for decades. The challenge of preparing regions for the long-term adaptability and resilience needed is obviously considerable and requires vision, priority setting for the use of limited resources, and cooperation at the regional and local level. It requires the ongoing commitment of both the public and private sectors, of both for-profit and nonprofit organizations. At the heart of the challenge is the need for leadership at all levels.

ULI is committed to being part of the process of meeting this challenge because it goes to the heart of ULI's mission "to provide leadership in the responsible use of land and in creating and sustaining thriving communities worldwide." ULI district councils—working with local members in partnership with members from around the world, as was done for this post-Sandy advisory panel—can provide needed leadership and partnership in regions around the United States and the world that are facing the impact of climate change and sea level rise.

The members of the post-Sandy panel and staff have worked hard together to make this panel and its report available. It is their hope that its insights and recommendations, though targeting the New York–New Jersey region, will be a valuable resource for other ULI district councils, as well as governments and organizations in other regions, as they engage in ongoing planning and development for the future. This work will never be finished, yet it is indispensable if our children and grandchildren are to enjoy the benefits of sustainable and thriving regions.

Notes

1 Intergovernmental Panel on Climate Change, *Fifth Assessment Report (AR5)* (Cambridge: Cambridge University Press, forthcoming).

2 "About the Hurricane Sandy Rebuilding Task Force," U.S. Department of Housing and Urban Development, http://portal.hud .gov/hudportal/HUD?src=/sandyrebuilding/about.

3 Ibid.

4 Biggert-Waters Flood Insurance Reform Act of 2012 (BW-12).

5 FEMA, "NFIP Policyholders: Total Number of Subsidized Policies by State and County (as of 12/31/2012)," http://www.arcgis.com /home/webmap/viewer.html?webmap=e0208985e8e64d44bca999325254ff5b&extent=-106.6909,33.1708,-76.9399,43.9898.

Participants and Interviewees

Sandy Advisory Services Panel

John K. McIlwain, Chair
Senior Resident Fellow/J. Ronald Terwilliger
  Chair for Housing
Urban Land Institute
Washington, D.C.

Joe Azrack, Cochair
Managing Partner
Apollo Global Real Estate
New York, New York

David M. Ricci, Cochair
Partner
The Flynn Company
Philadelphia, Pennsylvania

Panelists

Peter A. Angelides
Principal
Econsult Solutions Inc.
Philadelphia, Pennsylvania

Uwe S. Brandes
Executive Director, Master of Professional
  Studies in Urban and Regional Planning
School of Continuing Studies
Georgetown University
Washington, D.C.

Marc D. Brookman
Partner
Duane Morris LLP
Philadelphia, Pennsylvania

Joseph Brown
Chief Innovation Officer
AECOM
San Francisco, California

Kathleen Carey
Executive Vice President and Chief
  Content Officer
Urban Land Institute
Washington, D.C.

Tom Cox
Community Revitalization Consultant
Pittsburgh, Pennsylvania

Kristina Ford
Professor of Professional Practice in International
  and Public Affairs
Columbia University
New York, New York

Christopher M. Hager
Principal and Vice President
Langan Engineering & Environmental Services
Philadelphia, Pennsylvania

Steven Horowitz
Attorney
Cleary, Gottlieb, Steen & Hamilton LLP
New York, New York

Debra Lam
Associate, Cities and Climate Change
Arup
New York, New York

William Lashbrook
Senior Vice President
PNC Bank
East Brunswick, New Jersey

Stanley Lowe
President and CEO
Pittsburgh Neighborhood Preservation Services
Pittsburgh, Pennsylvania

James F. Murley
Executive Director
South Florida Regional Planning Council
Hollywood, Florida

Tom Murphy
Senior Resident Fellow/Klingbeil Family
  Chair for Urban Development
Urban Land Institute
Washington, D.C.

Ellen Neises
Department of Landscape Architecture
Graduate School of Design
University of Pennsylvania
Philadelphia, Pennsylvania

Corinne Packard
Clinical Assistant Professor
NYU Schack Institute of Real Estate
New York, New York

Richard W. Reynolds
Senior Adviser to the Executive Vice President
Tufts University
Boston, Massachusetts

Ommeed Sathe
Vice President, Social Investments
Prudential Financial
Newark, New Jersey

Byron Stigge
Director
Level Infrastructure
Brooklyn, New York

Marilyn Taylor
Dean
University of Pennsylvania School of Design
Philadelphia, Pennsylvania

Lynn Thurber
Chairman
LaSalle Investment Management
Chicago, Illinois

Pablo Vaggione
Director
Design Convergence
Madrid, Spain

ULI Staff

Susan Baltake
Executive Director
ULI Philadelphia
Haddonfield, New Jersey

Gayle Berens
Senior Vice President, Education and Advisory Group
Washington, D.C.

Annie Finkenbinder Best
Director, Education and Advisory Group
Washington, D.C.

Felix Ciampa
Executive Director
ULI New York
New York, New York

Kathryn Craig
Associate, Education and Advisory Group
Washington, D.C.

Caroline Dietrich
Logistics Manager, Education and Advisory Group
Washington, D.C.

Thomas Eitler
Vice President, Advisory Services
Washington, D.C.

Katrina Flora
Intern, Content Group
Washington, D.C.

Steven Gu
Intern, Education and Advisory Group
Washington, D.C.

Sarah Krautheim
Manager
ULI New York
New York, New York

Gerri Lipp
Director
ULI Philadelphia
Philadelphia, Pennsylvania

Daniel Lobo
Manager, Awards
Washington, D.C.

Mara Winoker
Manager
ULI Northern New Jersey
Montebello, New York

Interviewees

The panel thanks the more than 100 individuals in three locations who gave their time to be interviewed. Their expertise and opinions were invaluable to the panel.

LONG ISLAND

Michael Adamo
Development Manager
AvalonBay Communities

Nat Bottigheimer
Transportation Policy Adviser
HUD Sandy Task Force

Jon Cameron
Managing Partner
Cameron Engineering

Anthony Carvalho
Assessment Manager
Healthy Living Associates

Gerard Cattani
Assistant Superintendent
Planning Department
Garden City, New York

Margaret Davidson
Director
NOAA Coastal Services

Amy Engel
Executive Director
Sustainable Long Island

Michael Filippon
Superintendent
Planning Department
Garden City, New York

Robert Freudenberg
Director
Long Island and New Jersey Regional
  Plan Association

Christina Galante
Broker
Prudential Douglas Elliman

Marianne Garvin
President and CEO
Community Development Corporation

Rick Gropper
Project Manager
L+M Development Partners

Mike Hall
Principal
Arup

Glenda Hood
Cofounder
triSect LLC

Charles Lavine
Assemblyman
New York State Assembly

Julie Marchesella
President
Nassau Council of Chambers of Commerce

Jim Margo
Economic Adviser
Long Island Association

Betty Massey
Executive Director
Mary Moody Northern Endowment

Jonathan Miller
President and CEO
Miller Samuel

Bruce Reingold
Market Manager
Hunts Point Market

Jennifer Rimmer
Northeast Director of Strategic Initiatives
  and Sustainability
AECOM

Jack Schnirman
City Manager
City of Long Beach, New York

Laura Schwanof
Landscape Architect and Senior Ecologist
GEI Consulting

Jon Siebert
Member
Friends of Long Island

Al Smith
President
Breezy Point Cooperative

Wayne Wink
Legislator
Nassau County Legislature

Nathan Woiwode
Policy Adviser
The Nature Conservancy

NEW JERSEY

Thomas Barton
Principal
Barton Partners

Lori Buckelew
Senior Legislative Analyst
New Jersey State League of Municipalities

Jon Carnegie
Executive Director
Alan M. Voorhees Transportation Center

Chris Daggett
President
The Dodge Foundation

Thomas Dallessio
Resilient Design Project Manager
New Jersey Institute of Technology

James Florio
Former Governor
State of New Jersey

Lorena Gaibor
Sandy Rebuilding Coordinator
Housing and Community Development
  Network of New Jersey

Robin Ginsberg
Senior Vice President
Government and Institutional Banking
Wells Fargo

John Gray
Executive Assistant to the Deputy Commissioner
Department of Environmental Protection

Richard Johnson
Partner
Matrix Development Group

Marjorie Kaplan
Associate Director
Climate and Environmental Change Initiative
Rutgers University

Peter Kasabach
Executive Director
New Jersey Future

Brian Kelly
Member
Borough of Sea Bright Council
Chair
Sea Bright Recovery and Master Plan,
  Beautification

Joseph Kelly
President
Greater Atlantic City Chamber

Stephen Kirby
Cofounder
Community Healthcare Associates

Lance Landgraf
Principal Planner
Marathon Engineering and Environmental
  Services Inc.

Frank Lawrence
Coordinator
Sea Bright Resource Center

Corey Long
Project Executive
Bertino and Associates

Jay Lynch
Township Planner
Toms River

Tony MacDonald
Director
Urban Coast Institute
Monmouth University

Mark Mauriello
Director
Environmental Affairs and Planning
Edgewood Properties

Rachel Minnery
Regional Program Manager
Architecture for Humanity

Michael Redpath
President
Downtown New Jersey

Paul Smith
Mayor
Union Beach, New Jersey

Christopher Strom
Director of Project Development
AthenianRazak

Jessica Sweet
Founder and Principal
J.L. Sweet LLC
Chair
ULI Northern New Jersey

Linda Weber
Founding Principal
Mosaic Partners

NEW YORK CITY

Richard Anderson
President
New York Building Congress

Jacob Balter
Regional Transportation Planner
Long Island Railroad

Linda Baran
President and CEO
Staten Island Chamber of Commerce

Cynthia Barton
Housing Recovery Plan Manager
New York City Office of Emergency Management

Eddie Bautista
Executive Director
New York Environmental Justice Alliance

Vicki Been
Director
Furman Center for Real Estate and Urban Policy
New York University

Gillian Blake
Principal
Arup

Jeff Blau
CEO
The Related Companies

Alexander Brash
President
National Parks Conservation Association

Stuart Brodsky
Professor
Shack Institute for Real Estate
New York University

Cia Buckley
Chief Investment Officer
Dune Real Estate Partners

Amanda Burden
Commissioner
New York City Department of City Planning

Linda Conrad
Director of Strategic Business Risk
Zurich

Rebecca Craft
Director of Energy Efficiency Programs
ConEd

Susannah Drake
Principal
dlandstudio

Andrew Flamm
Economic Development Program Specialist
Empire State Development

Paul Freitag
Director of Rose Development
Jonathan Rose Companies

Mark Ginsberg
Principal
Curtis + Ginsberg Architects

Diana Glanternik
Assistant Vice President
New York City Housing Development
  Corporation

Joseph Gunset
General Counsel
Lloyd's

Samuel Hornick
Strategic Consultant
New York City Department of City Planning

Brooks Jackson
Senior Director for Policy and Research
Partnership for New York

Craig Johnson
Partner
McKenna & Aldridge

Samantha Kappagoda
Visiting Scholar
Courant Institute of Mathematical Sciences
New York University

Roland Lewis
President and CEO
Metropolitan Waterfront Alliance

Thomas Maguire
Assistant Commissioner
New York City Department of Transportation

Charlotte Matthews
Vice President, Sustainability
The Related Companies

Peter Miscovich
Managing Director
Strategy and Innovation
Jones Lang LaSalle

David Mordecai
Visiting Scholar
Courant Institute of Mathematical Sciences
New York University

Shola Olatoye
Vice President and Market Leader
Enterprise Community Partners

Henk Ovink
Senior Adviser to Secretary Shawn Donovan
Department of Housing and Urban Development

Mehul Patel
Chief of Staff
Empire State Development

Jerilyn Perine
Executive Director
Citizens Housing Planning Commission

Angela Pinsky
Senior Vice President
Real Estate Board of New York

Seth Pinsky
President
New York City Economic Development
   Corporation

Griffin Reilly
Engineer
ConEd

Mark Ricks
Chief Operating Officer
New York City Special Initiative for Rebuilding
   and Resiliency

Gerard Romski
Project Executive
Arverne by the Sea

Richard Rosan
President
ULI Foundation

Tokumbo Shobowale
Chief Business Operations Officer
City of New York

Howard Slatkin
Director of Sustainability
New York City Department of City Planning

Steven Spinola
President
Real Estate Board of New York

Jamie Springer
Principal
HR&A Advisors

Joan Tally
Executive Vice President for Real Estate
New York City Housing and Development
   Corporation

Kellie Terrey
Executive Director
The Point CDC

Ernest Tollerson
Director
Environmental Sustainability and Compliance
Metropolitan Transportation Authority

Alex Weinberg
Structural Engineer
Yolles/CH2M Hill

William Wheeler
Director
Special Projects and Planning
Metropolitan Transportation Authority

Kathryn Wylde
President and CEO
Partnership for New York

Tour Guides

Robert Antonicello
Executive Director
Jersey City Redevelopment Agency

Nate Bliss
Senior Vice President
New York City Economic Development
  Corporation

Connie Chung
Senior Planning Assistant
Alliance for Downtown New York

Bob Cotter
Planning Director
Jersey City

Nick Dmytryszyn
Environmental Planner
Office of the Staten Island Borough President

Christina Galante
Broker
Prudential Douglas Elliman

Rick Gropper
Project Manager
L+M Development Partners

Victoria Hagman
Founder and Owner
The Realty Collective

Tony MacDonald
Director
Urban Coast Institute, Monmouth University

Steve Marks
Business Administrator
City of Hoboken

Alison McKenna
Federal Emergency Management Agency

John McNally
Friends of Long Island

Brandon Mitchell
New York City Housing Recovery Office

Gerry Romski
Attorney
Beechwood Organization

Fred Sham
Senior Planning Analyst
Alliance for Downtown New York

Jon Siebert
Friends of Long Island

Al Smith
President
Breezy Point Co-op

Jon Tooke
Public Safety Director
City of Hoboken

Resources

Administration of Barack Obama. "Establishing the Hurricane Sandy Rebuilding Task Force." Exec. Order No. 13632, December 7, 2012. http://www.gpo.gov/fdsys/pkg/DCPD-201200936/pdf/DCPD-201200936.pdf.

Aerts, Jeroen C.J.H., and W.J. Wouter Botzen. "Flood-Resilient Waterfront Development in New York City: Bridging Flood Insurance, Building Codes, and Flood Zoning." *Annals of the New York Academy of Sciences* 1227 (2011): 1–82. doi: 10.1111/j.1749-6632.2011.06074.x.

American Institute of Architects New York, Post-Sandy Initiative. *Building Better, Building Smarter: Opportunities for Design and Development.* May 2013. http://postsandyinitiative.org/wp-content/uploads/2013/05/Post-Sandy-Report_Full.pdf.

Bloomberg, Michael R., Jeffrey D. Sachs, and Gillian M. Small. "Climate Change Adaptation in New York City: Building a Risk Management Response." *Annals of the New York Academy of Sciences* 1196 (2010): 1–3. doi: 10.1111/j.1749-6632.2009.05415.x.

Brandes, Uwe, and Alice LeBlanc. *Risk & Resilience in Coastal Regions.* Washington, DC: Urban Land Institute, 2013.

City of New York. *PlaNYC 2011 Update: A Greener, Greater New York.* 2011. http://nytelecom.vo.llnwd.net/o15/agencies/planyc2030/pdf/planyc_progress_report_2013.pdf.

Grannis, Jessica. *Adaptation Tool Kit: Sea Level Rise and Coast Land Use.* Washington, DC: Georgetown Climate Center, 2011. http://www.georgetownclimate.org/sites/default/files/Adaptation_Tool_Kit_SLR.pdf.

Heinz Center and Ceres. *Resilient Coasts: A Blueprint for Action.* Boston: Ceres, 2009. http://www.ceres.org/resources/reports/resilient-coasts-blueprint-for-action-2009/view.

Kenward, Alyson, Daniel Yawitz, and Urooj Raja. *Sewage Overflows from Hurricane Sandy.* Princeton, NJ: Climate Central, 2013. http://www.climatecentral.org/pdfs/Sewage.pdf.

Kuczinski, Tony, and Kenneth Irvin. *Severe Weather in North America: Perils, Risks, Insurance.* Munich, Germany: Munich Reinsurance America Inc., 2012. http://www.munichreamerica.com/pdf/ks_severe_weather_na_exec_summary.pdf.

Lloyd's. *Managing the Escalating Risks of Natural Catastrophes in the United States.* 2011. http://www.lloyds.com/~/media/lloyds/reports/emerging%20risk%20reports/natural%20catastrophes%20in%20the%20us.pdf.

Mathison, Christine. *Using Nature to Reduce Climate and Disaster Risks.* Arlington, VA: Nature Conservancy, 2012. http://coastalresilience.org/sites/default/files/resources/tnc_cc_UsingNature_v7b_web.pdf.

McHale, Cynthia, and Sharlene Leurig. *Stormy Future for U.S. Property/Casualty Insurers: The Growing Costs and Risks of Extreme Weather Events.* Boston: Ceres, 2012. http://www.ceres.org/resources/reports/stormy-future.

Metropolitan Transportation Authority, State of New York. *Greening Mass Transit & Metro Regions: The Final Report of the Blue Ribbon Commission on Sustainability and the MTA.* 2009. http://www.mta.info/sustainability/pdf/SustRptFinal.pdf.

Needelman, Brian, Stephen Crooks, Caroly Shumway, James G. Titus, Rich Tackacs, and Janet E. Hawkes. *2012 Restore-Adapt-Mitigate: Responding to Climate Change through Coastal Habitat Restoration.* Edited by B.A. Needelman, J. Benoit, S. Bosak, and C. Lyons. Washington, DC: Restore America's Estuaries, 2012. http://www.americaswetland.com/photos/article/rae%20climate%20chg%20report%204-19-2012.pdf.

New York–New Jersey Harbor & Estuary Program. "The New York–New Jersey Harbor Estuary Program: Roles and Recommendations as They Relate to Sandy and Planning for Resiliency to Future Coastal Storms." 2013. http://www.csi.cuny.edu/sandyforum/pdf/panel_3/NY-NJ+Harbor+Estuary+Program+roles+and+recommendations+for+DOI_Sandy.pdf.

New York State Sea Level Rise Task Force: Report to the Legislature. December 21, 2010. http://www.dec.ny.gov/docs/administration_pdf/slrtffinalrep.pdf.

New York State Senate. *Bipartisan Task Force on Hurricane Sandy Recovery: Preliminary Response & Recovery Report.* February 2013. http://www.nysenate.gov/report/bipartisan-task-force-hurricane-sandy-recovery-preliminary-report.

NYC Buildings. *Rebuilding NYC after Hurricane Sandy: A Guide to New Code and Zoning Standards for Industry Professionals.* June 2013. http://www.nyc.gov/html/dob/downloads/pdf/rebuilding_after_hurricane_sandy.pdf.

NYC Special Initiative for Rebuilding and Resiliency. *PlaNYC: A Stronger, More Resilient New York.* 2013. http://www.nyc.gov/html/sirr/html/report/report.shtml.

NYS 2100 Commission. *Recommendations to Improve the Strength and Resilience of the Empire State's Infrastructure.* 2013. http://www.governor.ny.gov/assets/documents/NYS2100.pdf.

Pirani, Rob, and Laura Tolkoff. *Building Capacity of Adaptive Planning after Sandy.* New York: Regional Plan Association, 2013. Draft.

Sandy Regional Assembly. "Sandy Regional Assembly Recovery Agenda: Recovery from the Ground Up—Strategies for Community-Based Resiliency in New York and New Jersey." April 2013. http://dl.dropboxusercontent.com/u/4969505/NYC-EJA/SandyRegionalAssemblyRecoveryAgenda_WEB_033013.pdf.

U.S. Green Building Council New York Chapter. *Building Resiliency Task Force: Report to Mayor Michael Bloomberg and Speaker Christine Quinn.* 2013. http://www.urbangreencouncil.org/BuildingResiliency.

Zurich Financial Services Group. *The Climate Risk Challenge: The Role of Insurance in Pricing Climate-Related Risks.* Zurich: Zurich Financial Services Group, 2009. http://www.zurich.com/sitecollectiondocuments/insight/climateriskchallenge.pdf.